- 2012

Praise for
Dick Cross and *Just Run It!*

"Business adviser Cross is a steadfast believer in the power of the American small business. Though half a million new businesses are founded each year, most fail because the founders lack the overarching knowledge of how to run a business. In response, Cross has developed a framework to structure the reader's thinking about how to tackle this challenge. He takes readers through the four dimensions that describe all businesses (needs, positioning, customers, and competencies), his process of Vision-Strategy-Execution, a business's natural life cycle, managing funds, and demystifying leadership and management, as well as offering scripts for discussions and negotiations, and tips for instituting values . . . a remarkably readable game plan for business success."   —*Publishers Weekly*

"Take a very bright architect who is trained to know how things 'fit.' Put him in positions of leadership where he invests the front half of his career as a consultant to CEO's and the back half actually being the CEO. . .and what do you get? One incredibly believable person. Read ***Just Run It!*** because it will benefit every company leader and provide personal gifts for a lifetime."
          —John C. Adams, Retired Chairman and CEO, AutoZone Inc.

"Save your time and money on consultants. Everything that Dick Cross shares with us comes from one of those rare generous birds who has taken the theoretical and applied it to real-time practice of running a company. ***Just Run It!*** is a must-read for anyone in management who is searching for strategic enlightenment."
          —Mike Toth, Founder and Chief Creative Director, Toth & Co

"Dick Cross's capacity to distill outwardly complicated concepts into comprehensible, value creating action steps is rare. Read the book . . . you'll learn something and be entertained."   —Peter Lamm, Fenway Partners

"Having owned, operated, and invested in many businesses over the years I can say that *Just Run It!* goes right to the core of running successful companies—outlining and explaining core platforms succinctly and with emphasis on fundamentals. Dick's focus is 'old school' in that people matter most, both on the inside and with customers/clients on the outside. *Just Run It!* presents a framework for businesses of all types in dramatically simple and easy-to-read fashion."

—Frederic H. Mayerson, Chairman, The Frederic H. Mayerson Group, The Walnut Group

"Just Run It! is a critical reference piece in assessing and managing every investment. The key to success is the best possible understanding up front, a clear vision of where a company can achieve value creation, and most importantly, an actionable plan. The Vision-Strategy-Execution approach allows for all of this while avoiding the number one mistake, hesitation to act."

—Robert Egan, Alston Capital Partners

"Dick Cross combines his real-world experience with his attention to design and architecture to examine the inherent structural dynamics of successful capital ventures. *Just Run It!* carries a universal message which is just as relevant to a small professional personal service business as it is to a large manufacturer of branded merchandise."

—Howell Hollis, Managing Partner, Smith Moore Law

"Just Run It! is the appropriate title for this book. I have had the opportunity to witness The Cross Method of running companies several times and have added this method to my consulting service for start-ups and mature companies and it has never failed me or my clients. Dick is one of those who have discovered the secret of combining passion with business, and his book teaches you to run your company by example."

—Thomas Gerety, Principal, Thomas F Gerety and Associates

"Dick Cross has a way of distilling complex ideas into simple to understand concepts. He then makes sure those simple ideas are constantly delivered to the organization and its constituents so that everyone understands what is possible. He instills a positive outlook in his work while creating an environment of integrity and values—in the process, building a committed team focused on achieving high and far reaching goals. Dick never accepts the status quo, but is always looking for ways to create a better, more understandable, more effective market-based business model."

—Douglas L. Diamond, Equity-South Advisors, LLC

Just Run It!

Just Run It!

Running an Exceptional Business Is Easier Than You Think

DICK CROSS

bibliomotion
books + media

First published by Bibliomotion, Inc.

33 Manchester Road
Brookline, MA 02446
Tel: 617-934-2427
www.bibliomotion.com

Printed in the United States of America

ISBN 978-1-937134-00-6

Library of Congress Control Number: 2012932286

Contents

Introduction

Your Timing Is Great

I completed the first draft of *Just Run It!* at the end of 2004. I didn't see then the coming downturn in the American economy. And I had no idea how much more appropriate the book would become as a result of that decline. But first, what happened between then and now?

The explanation I like best is the one put forth by the Scotsman William Hutchinson Murray in recounting his Himalayan expedition of 1951. In reflecting on the horrific challenges of unexpected weather and equipment failures on his ascent, and on how the hand of providence had guided him to do the right things at exactly the right times, he wrote:

> Until one is committed, there is hesitancy, the chance to draw back, always ineffectiveness. Concerning all acts of initiative (and creation), there is one elementary truth the ignorance of which kills countless ideas and splendid plans: that the moment one definitely commits oneself, then providence moves too. A whole stream of events issues from the decision, raising in one's favor all manner of unforeseen incidents, meetings and material assistance, which no man could have dreamt would have come his way.

In the case of *Just Run It!* the hand of providence moved twice since the end of 2004 to hold back the publication of the book until the circumstances of our economy were exactly right for its message.

The first act of providence was a telephone call I received, just as I'd finished the first draft, from a dear friend in the private equity world. The call was a request that I lead another intriguing company through a total transformation as its chairman and CEO. It took five years. But the experience added immeasurably to the war chest of stories and insights that now are embedded in the book.

The second act came just as that assignment was winding down. Bibliomotion, my publisher and my great support in shepherding the draft into an actual book, made an unsolicited inquiry through another friend about my unpublished manuscript. Out of the blue, five years after Bibliomotion's publisher had first heard about my book, she called. We met and hit it off famously.

I am most grateful for both of these interventions.

I am grateful because the unalterable truth is that right now the U.S. economy is struggling into the early stages of its first foundational transformation since the emergence of the Industrial Revolution at the end of the nineteenth century. That revolution, which catapulted the United States into its unchallenged position of global business and economic dominance, was based on two things: first, economies of scale in production, which we pioneered and then perfected through stateside efforts to support two World Wars; and second, our access to competitively priced, semi-skilled labor, raw materials, and capital.

Today, both of those competitive advantages have lost their punch. They've been superseded by new technologies that diminish the raw advantages of scale and by lower-cost labor as well as by governments' support of industry in other parts of the world. Giant production facilities, and the jobs associated with them, for making cars, heavy machinery, computer programming, clothing, furniture, cosmetics, packaging, basic materials, and the like are departing our shores. And they are not coming back.

But all is not lost. The inarguable truth is that the circumstances around all human endeavors change over time. And those with the foresight to change with the circumstances displace those who don't. Hard as it may be to digest, hanging onto our strategies of scale and cost advantage, which worked so convincingly in the past, has become a losing game plan. For those who can't adjust their thinking to new realities, the decline in America's global standing as an industrial power is a death knell. For those who can, it's the reveille of opportunity.

Now, a bit of good news in this picture is that the scale game isn't losing its punch only in the United States. It's already in the early stages of decline even in the places where it has just recently taken off. The spoils resulting from economies of scale and low-cost semi-skilled labor are diminishing everywhere, and the advantages accruing to those who have it now will be short lived. In America, we're just way ahead of most others in dealing with what's coming.

So, what does this mean for the future of business in the U.S.? It means that our new source of global advantage won't reside in mega-production, but rather in the proliferation and ingenuity of smaller enterprises. There are fresh opportunities to be found in the millions of experiments occurring every day, and businesses are moving quickly to uncover new advantages on hundreds of thousands of fronts. There's a new American financial and business infrastructure being built from the bottom up, and from the inside out—no longer will the most innovative businesses operate principally from the top down.

So, why isn't this happening faster? It's not because we lack freedom of enterprise in America. Nor does it stem from a paucity of ideas. It's not from a shortfall of initiative on the parts of would-be entrepreneurs, independent business owners, and workers either. It's not even from a scarcity of capital.

Roughly half a million new businesses start every year in the U.S., but most wither and disappear outright or fail to gain enough altitude to make much of a difference. Particularly these days, too many of our potentially powerful businesses languish in the zone between insolvency and subsistence and lock their owners and employees into lives of compromise and disappointment.

But, if we have no shortfall in ideas, initiative, capital, and other resources, why aren't things dramatically different? The answer is simple. And that answer lies at the heart of *Just Run It!* Businesses struggle because so few of the would-be drivers of the new economy know how to convert their dreams, their ideas, their courage, and their initiatives into successful businesses. They lack the overarching knowledge of *how to run a business*. This shortcoming is pervasive: it handicaps most new businesses from the start and it prevents the lion's share of existing ones from ever becoming significant. Learning *how to run a business* is just not yet a foundational element of our culture.

How to run a business, as a whole skill, is not yet talked about in business circles. It's not yet practiced in families. It's not considered in churches, school board meetings, or social groups as a way of living one's life. It's not taught in schools. Few people are ever exposed to solid role models who know how to do it. So it should be no surprise that few CEOs or company presidents ever think about the whole of their challenge. Rather, we remain obsessed with the Newtonian idea of examining only the parts in order to understand the universe. And, as the pace of change in the world around us accelerates, examining parts no longer constitutes a reliable and replicable approach to understanding and fixing the whole.

The *Just Run It!* philosophy is different. It does address the whole, the entirety of *how to run a business*. It's easy to understand. And even if you embrace its message with only a cursory level of commitment, it greatly increases the likelihood of your success and of your joy in the pursuit of your business. Beyond that, it offers you a framework and a discipline for enjoying a lifetime of refinement, fascination, and satisfaction running your business.

But the best news is that the effect doesn't stop with its benefits for you. Those who can apply the principles of *Just Run It!* are poised to unlock a new rush to global prominence for America, like the rush of the Industrial Revolution a hundred years ago, toward an entirely new global economic order. This new economic order will be anchored in the freedom of individual enterprise and driven by the spirit of independence and by the pioneering attitude upon which our nation was built.

The breakthrough ideas in *Just Run It!* aren't hard to understand. Nor are they hard to remember. When I use the principles outlined in this book in my speaking, coaching, running companies, and consulting, I find just the opposite. People get it immediately. The eyes-wide-open, "aha" moment is now predictable. The prescriptions of the Back of the Envelope and of Vision–Strategy–Execution that unfold on the following pages are easy to take. And with minimal effort, you will find the perspectives and the practices they introduce broadening and building themselves into the routines of your thought processes and into the patterns of your life.

Nonetheless, the hurdles we face in making the shift we need to make today, as individuals and as a nation, are significant. But I believe that they also are principally hurdles of will and of courage. We must be willing to leave old ways of doing things and be confident in their disappearing. We must have the courage to look forward with determination and optimism to building our lives as CEOs, presidents, and managers—along with the lives of those who work with us—according to new principles for success in the twenty-first century. If we do this, together we will lead the movement to the new economy, built from the bottom-up and not from the top-down, that our country, our communities, our employees, and our families so desperately need.

Thank you for deciding to read *Just Run It!* If you like it, talk about it with your friends, your colleagues, your employees, and your family. I'd love to hear from you, either when you're finished or along your way. I know that these simple principles can make a difference for you, and that with them you can make a difference in America.

I enjoyed writing *Just Run It!* for you, and I wish you all the best.

Chapter 1

The Challenge to Mainstream Businesses

With deep respect and a little nostalgia I look back at the 1990s and recall the first days of each year's Mid-Tier President's Course at Harvard. Shortly after the second break, a cloud would lift in the sanctuary of the classroom, after twenty or so CEOs, presidents, and general managers had revealed a hidden secret: No one had a clear idea about how to do his job.

More recently, it occurred to me that a related irony runs through many business books, the kinds of books that people who run businesses, or aspire to run them, read to relieve their anxieties. But a lot of those books have less relevance than we think, particularly those written by ex-Fortune 500 CEOs and their consultants that trade on a beguiling myth—the myth that the experiences from those people's careers are models for everyone else's. Most of the time, it just isn't so.

The lives of the people who run most of the businesses in America have as much to do with a Fortune 500 CEO's life as a sergeant's has to do with a czar's. Few of those authors ever tapped their own savings to meet a payroll, groveled at the local bank for a loan, filled in for a missing worker on the plant floor, or made a decision that damaged the life of a family with whom they shared Thanksgiving dinners, high school football games, or vacations at the lake.

There simply aren't many books for those of us who run mid-tier companies, the ones I call fondly the "mainstream" businesses of America. But this book is written precisely for those mainstream business owners. And it contains a prescription that works. Whether you are a twenty-year veteran, a first-timer, or are just thinking about the prospect of becoming a president or CEO, this book is for you. Whether your business is privately held, publicly traded, or a family enterprise, the upcoming chapters offer a proven guide for doing your job at the top and doing it well.

Is Yours A Mainstream Business?

Mainstream businesses anchor America's economic base. They're where half of Americans work, where most of our goods and services are produced, and where most of our country's money is made. I don't define them by sales volume or employee numbers. The main differentiator for me is that they can be run by a single individual under a single plan. They are "one-business" businesses.

We run mainstream businesses ourselves, whether our revenues are posted in the tens of thousands or tens of millions. We don't have general managers or large staffs. Hiring, firing, investing in new technologies, marketing, cost reduction, productivity, and the flow of funds and profits are our direct responsibilities. The range of tasks we cover every day eclipses our widely published counterparts' by tenfold; from employees' problems with their children and their car loans to redesigning capital structures and defending ourselves in lawsuits, we do it all. And most of us answer our own phones.

We are important. Our skill in our jobs has more to do with the well-being of American families than the performance of the entire Fortune 500 or any federal government program in history. But, most of us have never had formal training for our responsibilities. There aren't many books for us. And there are none that address the entirety of how to do our jobs.

Why Me, Why Now?

I remember the moment I decided to focus my career on understanding how to run mainstream businesses. It was a perfect springtime Saturday afternoon in New England. I was floating down a lazy river not far from my house, casting a fly to spawning swirls near the shore. I hadn't caught many fish, but it didn't matter. I'd finished a painting project that morning and my thoughts had wandered onto a transcendental theme. Manual work does that to me. It's one of the reasons I like it.

From the time I pulled off the shoulder of the ancient road next to the stream and began unstrapping the pudgy, little cedar-strip canoe from the old station wagon, I'd been really enjoying myself. I thought back over my life so far. I'd done my military service. I'd finished graduate school at the head of my class. I was in my third year as an up-and-comer in a prestigious management consulting firm, and I had the whole world in front of me.

My musings that day ran along the lines of: "How can I use the blessings I've received to greatest effect? How will I be able to make the greatest difference? How can I help the most people?" A medical career was out of the question. I'd finished my allotment of schooling, and I hadn't been a star in science. Though I had an interest in the church, training for the clergy had not been part of my preparation. I'd chosen instead an educational combination of design and business. My first few years of management consulting were spent carrying bags for revered senior Harvard Business School faculty and watching them fix companies. Their skills and their integrity had completely and joyfully won me over.

On the slow pick-up from an unproductive cast, I watched the lazy curl of the line roll out over my right shoulder. A thought occurred to me. In just three years of supporting these icons of business in their work, I'd developed an unusual perspective. I'd seen the insides of about fifty businesses by then. At the very moment my line straightened out and loaded the little cane rod behind me, I realized that if someone gave me the opportunity to spend a week just talking to people inside a company—any company— I could paint an accurate psychological portrait of the person in charge, without ever having met him.

I sat down in my small canoe. My mind went blank. I don't know how long I sat there, but when I started thinking again, I knew I'd found something important: direction. The understanding that unfolded for me in that instant was about the effect that the talents, motivations, character, and manner of the person in charge has on everyone associated with the business. The effect is pervasive. People don't even realize, while it is happening, the effect that the business leader's approach has on their every thought and action. And it is astounding to see.

I felt as if the previous ten years had all been leading up to this single, intense revelation. Looking back, I could see everything—my education, my jobs, my interests, my reading—that had prepared me for this spike. Looking forward, I could see my life marked indelibly by my newfound direction.

My mind raced. I felt like I'd been walking on a beach and found a huge diamond left behind in the receding surf. I was suddenly exhausted and exhilarated at the same time. What would I do with this jewel? The answer wasn't far away. It washed over me like a warm and friendly breeze. It left me deeply committed, entirely content, and grateful to be in its wake. I would spend my life learning how to run mainstream businesses and helping others learn how to run them too. This would be a life well spent. If I could do it well, I could contribute to the lives of tens of thousands, maybe hundreds of thousands, of others.

By the time I became aware again of the slim cork grip of the willowy cane in my hand, I'd drifted quite a ways in the mild current. Attached to the end of my line was a self-hooked, tired, small minnow of an undistinguished sort. I reeled him in slowly, gently removed the hook from the hole in his lip, released him to his freedom, and paddled back upstream toward the rest of my life. And, eventually, to yours.

What Nobody Knows

How do you run a business? It's a ubiquitous question. But also, it's one that is seldom asked. *Why?* Because, I think, no one really expects an answer.

Articles, seminars, tapes, DVDs, and webcasts flood us with advice on leadership, management, productivity, creating value, ethics, systems, and planning, but not on how to just *run* a business. Business schools aren't much better. To my knowledge, none offer a course entitled, "How to Run a Business." Yet, somehow, the aggregate of a two-year curriculum is supposed to deliver the answer, without ever addressing the question directly.

The secrets of running businesses remain sequestered among those who, first, have been fortunate enough to be selected for the job, and, second, have survived the experience. But even among those few, there is not much talk about a general approach to, or theory of, the whole job. Most struggle to find words to describe how they do what they do. Veteran leaders talk easily about parts of their jobs, and relate riveting war stories about incidents along the way, but it is the rare example who can distill her years of experience into a concise and comprehensive description that is helpful to others. And I think I know why.

Imprinting on Sir Isaac Newton's approach to scientific discovery, Western culture convolved an approach to science and problem solving that works from the bottom up. In addition to his discovery of gravity, recalled in the fabled story about the falling apple, Newton made other monumental advancements in mathematics, astronomy, and physics. But none of these were his primary intention. Instead, Newton's life of scientific achievement was simply the by-product—steps along the way—of his deeply religious passion to discover the greater rationale of his God's universe. And the method he chose was to examine its component parts. It is this approach—looking at the parts to understand the whole, rather than the astounding individual breakthroughs he made along the way—that set in place a new model for analytic thought that endures today. Rather than thinking about the entirety of a phenomenon, we, following Newton's model, also disaggregate complex things into their component parts and then study the parts for clues about what makes the whole "tick." Our presumption is that if we understand all of the pieces, we can understand, de facto, the whole. To fix a broken whole, we find the flawed piece, fix it, reassemble the parts, and expect the whole to work. Physics, medicine, automobile mechanics, and even many of the social sciences work this way. So, we probably shouldn't be surprised when we ask someone how he runs a business and his answer addresses only a part of the question. However, I find this disturbingly unsatisfying.

Just Run It! offers a different answer. It is a theory of the whole that grew out of my nearly thirty years of running mainstream businesses, reflecting on and studying the experiences, and teaching others how to do it.

Watershed ideas emerge from time to time that contribute powerful insights into certain aspects of running a business, but all fall short of addressing the whole. Occasionally, one takes hold for a while and has great influence on the way businesses are run during that time. Each adds something to an ever growing, but still unconsolidated, body of knowledge.

As examples, Boston Consulting Group's Growth-Share Matrix dominated business thinking through the mid- and late 1970s. It is still a wonderful idea; it's now largely passé, though. No one talks about Dogs and Stars any more. Michael Porter's Competitive Strategy then took the stage. After Porter came Re-engineering. A decade later the Total Quality movement displaced them all. Then the buzz sounded from Japan on Lean. And the pattern will go on. And it is likely to keep yielding the same result, with every new idea adding something to the toolkit, but none addressing the whole of how to run a mainstream business.

I believe that this book, like Newton's breakthrough model for analytic thinking, provides a new way for using all of these ideas—those of the past and those yet to come—to better understand the whole of *how to run a business*. The secret is an overarching framework that structures our thinking about how to run a business and that helps us select the right ideas in the right sequences, in the right measures, and at the right times.

The pages that follow will show you how to accomplish that dizzying goal.

Chapter 2

Your Business on the Back of an Envelope

Here is where the framework for running your mainstream business begins. In this chapter I will introduce you to the first of two frameworks, with one additional and overarching idea to follow. Together, these three concepts offer an innovative way of thinking about your business, but they are also soundly proven tools for evaluating all the business ideas you will encounter. They will give you a solid foundation for judging which tools to implement when, and in which sequence. And finally, you will learn a lot about how to put them to work for you, addressing the real issues in your company.

The Back of the Envelope Framework

Most businesses start because someone has an idea for a service or a product that others will pay enough for to cover the costs and leave a profit. Embodied in this simple notion of cost/profit is the fundamental logic that lies at the core of every business. It sounds pretty simple, right? It is. And over the next few pages I'll outline the right first steps for starting to think about it clearly. Applied against the "counterpunching" we all do—responding to things other than those we intended to do over the course of the workday—this simple framework helps you stay centered on the fundamentals of your business and on using your time and your thinking to continuously protect and improve them.

Here's how I first came up with the initial framework: Late one night about twenty years ago, I was on an airplane headed home from a consulting engagement. I was thinking about why there was no simple and universal way of describing businesses. Why was there no way that allowed people to maintain their focus on the things that really mattered?

As I thought, I sketched the back of an envelope on a writing pad. I thought about how a single sheet of paper could be folded four times to create a container that could hold all sorts of great ideas. Depending on the size of the paper and upon the geometry of the folds, the product could take any number of dimensions. Yet through all its variations and regardless of its contents, it remained an envelope. I mused over the standard number 10 envelope I had sketched on my pad, and it hit me: Each of the triangles formed by the folds represented one of four dimensions that, taken together, describe all businesses. The four are: customers, needs, positioning, and competencies.

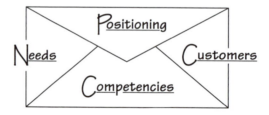

Customers

Who, specifically, are the intended customers for your business? Most businesses turn to demographics for their answers, and come up with things like:

> Middle-income women in the Northeast seeking affordable care for their children, ages 2–5, during working hours.

But only rarely does this kind of description anchor a really successful business. Why? Because it misses the most important thing you need to know about customers in order to become their preferred choice, particularly these days. Today, that most important thing has a lot more to do with how customers think versus where they live, their incomes, whether they own or rent their homes, how many children they have, their ages, and their ethnicities.

Today, through social networking and the Internet, customers of all demographics can find acceptable substitutes for nearly every product or service imaginable, with comparable levels of convenience and pricing. As a result, slowly but surely, many products in the United States are being commoditized, with multitudes of choices nearly indistinguishable from one another.

Exacerbating this commoditization of goods and services is a decline of materialism that is occurring across many segments of the American population, due in part to recent and broad global economic shifts. The other part of the equation is a growing understanding that material accomplishment doesn't ensure happiness. Accordingly, material things mean less to many people, particularly younger adults looking at the reality of lives that are more challenging, financially, than the ones their parents lived. Researchers dealing with young adult consumers are finding that aspirations like having friends and living principled lives rank ahead of acquiring possessions in many of their surveys. And people's senses of themselves and their expected realities powerfully influence how they behave as customers. So, it's no longer sufficient to define customers according to who they are, how much money they have, and where they live. The operative differentiator now is how they think. And many are thinking differently than they were just a few years ago.

Begin your "Back of the Envelope" exercise by categorizing customers according to how they think. If your business approaches your customers through an accurate understanding of how they think, rather than who they are and what you sell, you will tap in to the things they really care about. And you will see new opportunities to build a strong platform for intense loyalty, repeat business, and referrals.

The most influential businesses over the past five to ten years get this. They are the ones aligning themselves most precisely with the emotional make-ups and thought patterns of their customers. They are the ones who touch their customers in ways above and beyond the actual services and products they provide. It has long been said that people buy from people—

and they especially buy from people they like and who demonstrate that they understand and care about their customers.

Make a list of what's important to your target customers. These things don't need to have anything to do with your offering. Then arrange your list in descending order of what they'd be willing to give up. Things like health and family are probably going to be at the top. Keep going until you get to whatever it is that you provide. The exercise can be a humbling experience. But at least you'll know where you stand. And you may discover some things that you could add, often at no additional cost, to improve the attractiveness of your offering, so customers will prefer you over their other alternatives. Acting on these kinds of insights, gained from "standing in your customers' moccasins" for a while, can become a powerful differentiator in the minds of your intended audience. It will also serve you well in our later discussion on competitive positioning.

Needs

If you've done a good job of defining your target customers according to how they think, you've already started considering their needs in general terms. Now you have to get specific. What do your target customers need that is within your zone of influence? Think beyond what you already do and how you do it. How can you satisfy them better than any of your competitors? And how can you differentiate yourself in their minds so compellingly that they will consider no other choice? How can you do it in ways that your competitors can't match? These are big questions. Remember, though, that nearly every example of satisfying needs boils down to just two simple ideas: reducing fear or making people feel better about themselves.

Building upon what you've identified about what's important in the lives of your target customers, make two more lists. On one, record their fears that you might be able to do something about. On the other, list the opportunities you have to make them feel better about themselves. Go back over the lists to see where the two intersect, and write down specific things you might be able to do to resolve needs that appear on both lists.

Test your findings by asking whether fulfilling those needs would make your target customers select your business. Then confirm whether the "yes" answers are within your capability and whether supplying that item or service would result in revenues that exceed the costs.

This exercise usually takes a number of trials before it yields a set of "yeses" that survive the tests. But they always exist, for every business. Most of us just aren't accustomed to thinking this way.

Note that many business heads make the mistake of assuming that their own needs for emotional satisfaction match those of their customers. Solid business leaders understand that it's their customers' value systems that count, and they tailor every aspect of their business to deliver effective match-ups with their customers' thought processes. Some even find their own satisfaction, and their fascination with their businesses, rising as they begin to understand more fully their customers' make-ups and begin to see their customers not as "targets" but as their partners in a meaningful life of enterprise.

Positioning

So far, we've been talking about who your customers are according to how they think and you've made some initial choices about which of your customers' needs you are going to be best at satisfying. So far, all of this has been about what you can do on the inside of your business to influence its course.

Now the process turns outside. How does your business need to be "seen" by outsiders? How will it become "known?" What messages will you convey? And how will you stand behind those messages so your target customers will consider your business as their first choice among their set of acceptable alternatives?

Logos, brochures, advertising, and packaging that talk about what you do can help, certainly, and these should tie in to accurate understandings of how your customers think and what they need. But increasingly, other modes of messaging are launching and sustaining "the buzz" that attracts today's more sophisticated buyers. The most powerful formats are testimonial stories that relate what it's like to deal with your business. These testimonials mean the most when they come from people not directly associated with your business. Independent endorsements about how it feels to do business with you beat paid advertising, in my experience, by a margin of about ten to one.

A single, powerfully positive testimonial on Facebook influences thousands with credible messaging about your business. But one negative comment can turn tens of thousands away, forever. Today, engaging new customers through others who have been impressed with things you've done that go beyond satisfying their immediate needs is your most potent weapon in winning their business.

So, what are the right messages? These days, the most effective messages through nearly all media are less centered on the facts, features, and prices of your products or services. Instead, they focus on who you are. Because so many products and services are now seen as commodities, customers are increasingly looking to build "relationships" with businesses they can trust. They're looking to you, as the face of your business, to help reduce a personal fear or make them feel better about themselves. As good as you believe your products or services may be, the facts and features alone are rarely enough to seal the deal with discerning customers. They want to feel that they're being taken care of by someone who understands them. Your stongest position is to become one of those rare persons they can trust to make meaningful contributions in satisfying those longings.

What kindles and then builds these kinds of relationships? It's a range of things, including some so small that we usually overlook them. At the other end of the range are things so extraordinary that they become hits on YouTube.

Anchoring the small end of the range are things like the way you answer the phone or greet your customers as they enter, whether you send thank-you notes, and whether you support a charity your customers care about. Recently, at a business I worked with, I insisted that front office personnel stand up and walk forward to greet every customer who crossed the thresh-old. The idea was to tell our customers how glad we were that they chose us and to ask them how we could help them. If we weren't positioned to satisfy their needs, we'd offer to help them find someone else who was.

In the middle of the spectrum are the traditional elements of the marketing mix: your website; the look of your storefront, parking lot, and public spaces; the way employees dress; the look of your packaging; your advertising and promotions; and the generosity of your warranty policy.

For example, I've loaded websites with simple but glowing customer video testimonials, taken with simple equipment right in the shop. The casual atmosphere adds authenticity. Most people love being asked to do this, and they do a great job. I've put welcome signs with different greetings on posts at every customer parking space. I've added premium coffee (if you're not willing to spring for great coffee, don't do it at all, because nothing says "I don't care about you" louder than stale coffee), fresh, unexpected snacks, flat screen televisions, and Wi-Fi in customer waiting spaces. I have instituted peer review visits, where the operator of one business visits another and notes the little things that people who are present every day tend to overlook, like cracks in the sidewalk, wilting shrubs, fingerprints on glass doors and windows, and less-than-perfect, fresh-smelling bathrooms with full rolls of toilet tissue.

The blockbusters are the massive efforts you didn't have to do to satisfy a need. They're instances when you choose to go way beyond what someone paid for just to be nice, and the gesture gets picked up by the evening news.

At CARSTAR, an international automobile repair franchise company, I restored a famous muscle car from the 1960s and toured it as the centerpiece for a company-wide charitable commitment for sick kids. We also raised funds at golf tournaments, car shows, car washes, and cruise nights that we hosted with our franchise owners across the country. With every completed repair, we gave the customer a certificate documenting the donation we made in his name from the proceeds of our repair work. This simple act of doing something good on behalf of our customer, which extended beyond what was expected and paid for, beat the effectiveness of all our other advertising in generating local and trade news coverage, consumer awareness, community good will, referrals, and customer loyalty. That was a blockbuster.

When you encourage and perform these kinds of acts across the entire spectrum—small to blockbuster—and with an explicit consciousness about matching who you are to the way your customers think, you build a "third dimension"—a persona—for your business. And increasingly, customers are looking to spend their money with businesses that have personas they like and trust. These are the businesses to which customers want to "award" their purchases, and with whom they seek to build long-standing and loyal relationships.

At this point, you've written down who your customers are according to how they think and you've enumerated what they need. Looking back over what you've recorded, make a list of all the things you could be doing—your potential actions—to convey to them who you are in terms of how they think, under three headings: small, medium, and blockbuster.

If most of what you're already doing lines up pretty well with your list, you're a lot better off than most businesses. Where you've got some open bases, assign a rating of 1 to 5 to reflect the degree of difficulty and cost you believe might be associated with covering each one. Then assign another rating of 1 to 5, based on the impact you believe each initiative will have on building a more positive impression with your customers. Subtract the first number from the second. The resulting 4s and 5s, and maybe even some of the 3s, are things you really need to consider doing. You'll be surprised by how many there are.

Competencies

So far we've talked about ideas. In this last quadrant of the envelope, we'll talk in tangible terms about your business, about the capabilities and resources you'll need to act on the logic built up in the other three triangles of the envelope. What skills does it actually take to deliver the goods, to do the things you'd like to promise, and not to disappoint anyone? The broken promise is the kiss of death for your business and word of it spreads like wildfire.

In my work with over a hundred companies, what I have found is that most peoples' first lists are things that all businesses ought to do—keep up with innovations in the industry, deliver value, outperform their competition, and stand behind their products. These are all useful, but they're not sufficient. It takes multiple passes through the first three triangles of the Back of the Envelope to get to the real stuff. But once you're there, be sure that you're ready to act on your words before you offer them to your audience.

The best businesses tailor every aspect of their existence—from their products and services to the look of their business space and materials to the behavior of company representatives—to match the thinking patterns, needs, and emotional profiles of their targeted customers. This is the perspective that adds energy to the whole exercise. Without it, the Back of the Envelope is just words. With it, the Envelope becomes an article of faith.

These kinds of businesses know that their competence in touching their customers in all the ways their competitors don't builds and sustains their relationships. They also know that customers who are treated like they're special tell others: sometimes they talk about something as simple as the warm greeting when they enter your office or the fresh cup of coffee that they'd pay two dollars for elsewhere. Other times, they talk about how you sent a thank-you note. Or it's about how you offered to extend a service and courtesy beyond what they paid for. The best business leaders know that the relationships they work consciously to develop with their customers—built around their understanding of how those customers think and what they need and around how the business is positioned in customers' minds—are the keys to superior growth and security.

So get out the lists you've made, review your scorings of 3 to 5 (the difference between the ranked effects of what you might do differently and their costs), and decide what, specifically, you need to do and what resources you need to deploy in order to create the business persona that will attract and keep your customers.

Your to-do list might include refining or redesigning your products, shortening response times, retraining customer contact personnel, or restructuring pricing. But it also ought to include things like making your employees feel great about your business. Touch them with compelling acts and messages that back up what you say and that reinforce how you'd like them to interact with your customers.

In this last triangle you'll find the hardest challenge in the Back of the Envelope framework. It's the part that sends nearly everyone back to the very beginning of the process at least once. This is the reality check on whether you actually possess, or can obtain, the resources—the people, technology, systems, processes, products, creativity, pricing, and cost structure—to make your Back of the Envelope story a reality.

Be brutally honest in this fourth triangle, this last acid test. But don't be dissuaded after your first run through the Back of the Envelope process if the answer is no, if you can't afford what you'd like to do. It usually turns out this way for a while in the early going. But "no" is actually a good finding, because it prevents you from wasting time and saves you from failure. Continue cycling through the process, and eventually you will come to a Back of the Envelope construction that makes inarguable sense in terms of its match with the way your customers think and in terms of its doability. Don't be surprised or dismayed if it turns out to be a far cry from what you are doing today. Death by slow attrition, from striving ever harder to execute a losing game plan, is a bad way to go.

I've run this "Back of the Envelope" process with hundreds of businesses over the past two decades. Sometimes it takes us a day. Sometimes, it takes months. Your timeframe will depend on the complexity of your current business, the number of people who are involved in the discussion, and the trust that your team has in you and in one another.

In most instances, the results are the same: People are amazed at the findings. It's likely that you will be too. Typical responses include:

- Gee, when you look at it that way, it calls into question the value of a lot of the programs we've been counting on for quite some time.
- Now I understand why pouring more and more resources into what made us successful in the past isn't working any more.
- I have a better understanding now of the tensions among our management team—people are simply arguing for different concepts about how to win.
- After really looking at our customers' needs, I see how Competitor X always beats us to the punch going after Customer Y.
- It's fun to think about aligning everything we do to build upon itself, rather than working at cross-purposes and taking shots in the dark.
- I see things now, important things, that we need to be doing as part of our business that I'd never even come close to considering before. I also see things we continue to do that make no sense.

As Professor Edgar Schien of the Alfred P. Sloan School of Management at MIT noted more than thirty years ago, the starting point for running a business well is an understanding of what business you are in. And, I would add, of what businesses you are not in. The Back of the Envelope is the best way I've found for defining this starting point and for keeping it fresh and "front-and-center" in your mind, in what is often a sea of compelling distractions. It is also the anchor point for the next framework in your toolkit for running your business.

Chapter 3

The Vision-Strategy-Execution Framework and How It Operates

The Back of the Envelope model is the starting point for thinking powerfully about how to run your business. But it's just the start. In this chapter, I will give you an overview of the second key framework, Vision–Strategy–Execution. This one builds on the work you did on the Back of the Envelope, and becomes the centerpiece for how to run your business. In the chapters that follow this one, we'll dig deeper into each component of this new centerpiece.

Never as a consultant, nor as an advisor, nor as a CEO has this simple, three-part logic, which I am about to share with you, let me down. In fact, without its guiding principle as my compass, I am sure that I would have failed most of the time. You can think of the three parts of this model as three different styles of thinking about your business. I liken them to wearing tri-focal lenses, which allow you to constantly shift between three fields of view and maintain clear vision all the while.

Each part needs to be done well, and they all need to be synchronized. Furthermore, this model needs to spread throughout your organization to the point where it is at least understood, if not held in conscious thought, by everyone, from those who conduct the annual shareholders' meeting to the newest hires on the plant floor. For that to be possible, it can't be complicated or long. The entire three-part prescription needs to be distilled into a few clear and powerful ideas. And it should be able to be encapsulated on just a few pages. The thinking that winds up on those few short pages becomes the template for a hopefully life-fulfilling practice of continual reflection, refinement, and self-improvement.

Lots of the most satisfying things in life work that way. Yoga, for example, is a pretty straightforward set of body positions coupled with a discipline for breathing and relaxation. Limbering up enough to assume the basic stances is hard enough at first. Perfecting the techniques and exploring the boundaries of their influences, however, can be the joyous work of a lifetime.

The three-part approach for running a business is like yoga in that way. The model looks simple, but within it is embedded a lifetime of personal challenge, growth, and, most importantly, service for everyone associated with your business.

Many people even casually familiar with the last twenty or so years of business literature might be tempted to say, "Yeah, I already know what that's all about. I've just never really seen it drawn that way," and move on. But my experience is that almost everyone who takes the time to dig a little deeper into these ideas and to understand how they truly can work together becomes fascinated with the subtleties and complexities they involve—and, like yoga, these ideas can help not only with how you run a business, but also with how to run a church group, a little league team, a family, or even your own life.

How It Happens

Conceptually, the logic of Vision–Strategy–Execution (V-S-E) builds from left to right. The arrows indicate that. Big picture to little picture. Vision to execution. But in reality, businesses almost never build up that way. Usually, it's the reverse. Right to left. Backwards.

Almost nobody starts a business because she has a vision. Almost nobody derives a strategy out of an abstract vision. And few ever have the opportunity to start with a blank piece of paper to create an execution plan for the purpose of following through on a previously defined strategy.

Most businesses start because someone has what she believes to be an executable idea—which is hardly ever articulated in the context of the Back of the Envelope model. And some of these people get lucky. Why only some? Because 30 percent of all new businesses fail within the first two years. Fifty percent fail within the first four. And fewer than 30 percent survive after ten. Most of those that fail don't succumb because the owners and employees didn't work hard enough. Or because they weren't smart. Or because the basic idea for the business didn't make any sense. The failures occur because the businesses, when examined in the framework of the Back of the Envelope model, were flawed from the outset. For example:

- The reachable base of intended customers was too small to generate the required revenue stream.
- The customer needs that were identified turned out to be not so important to the customers, after all.
- Better-positioned relationships already existed in that market.
- Resources were either too modest to live up to the promise of the positioning, or the positioning achieved was not remarkable enough to distinguish the business from the rest of the pack.
- The resources of the business fell far short of what would have been required to convey convincingly the acutal merits of the offering to a large enough audience.
- The owner's evaluation of the quality of the offering was, in fact, a mismatch with what customers actually wanted.

Execution

For those businesses that do reach solvency, with a solid Back of the Envelope model in place before their initial capital runs out, whether they continue or fail beyond their initial points of survival usually depends upon how well they execute their business model. "Quality of execution" here refers to the diligence, creativity, and precision with which the business lives its Back of the Envelope model—day to day, week to week, and quarter to quarter, person by person.

I hear enraptured remembrances about how founders' businesses consumed their lives in their early years. Joyously so. They rhapsodize about multitasking, thinking on their feet, paying attention to every detail, with everyone in the organization striving for the same mark, covering one another's backs, and improving every day, infused with a maniacal zeal to outperform the competition. The entire force of the business launched foward to develop a business persona that honored relationships based on satisfying a set of clearly articulated needs for a thoughtfully defined set of customers.

Teaching people how to execute like this was pretty much what business research and education were all about through the 1960s. Lessons from World War II about how to manufacture and distribute products efficiently—how to get and keep large numbers of people focused on the same goal, with each doing his predetermined part of the job, and how to track it all with numbers—were retooled for civilian application. And in the retooling, a whole body of scholarship, referred to as the new "science" of management, emerged from the halls of the leading business schools of America. This new science allowed business leaders to apply statistics to hundreds of subfunctions that had to be coordinated in order to execute a Back of the Envelope business idea. Today, we have lots of tools for doing this.

However, every business reaches a point when harder, more diligent, and even more clever execution of the existing Back of the Envelope business model begins to yield continuously diminishing returns. The pipeline of demand for the original offering is filled. Growth is reduced to replacement. New technologies and better alternatives come along. Customers' tastes and emotional needs change. And most business owners and managers know it when these things are happening.

But despite their knowledge that their businesses are stagnating, too many view the uncertainty and the risk associated with abandoning what worked in the past as insurmountable barriers. I've talked to hundreds of captains of failing businesses, and nearly all of them knew what they needed to do in order to avoid a regrettable outcome. Their inabilities to act on what their instincts and their intellects told them were the turning points that sank their businesses into steady states of decline. Like biological organisms, businesses that fail to adapt to their changing circumstances cease to exist. Also, in nearly every case of business failure, there's a double whammy of hindsight. The person in charge not only knew what he needed to do, but doing it at the right time wouldn't have been all that difficult!

We'll talk more later about effective execution through the life of a business. But for now, the key point to remember about execution is that it is a continually moving target. As soon as we get comfortable with how things are going, we may have already passed the best point for changing them. And it takes a special culture to foster the kind of behavior that adapts instinctively. Creating that kind of adaptive culture is a key role for the person at the top. We'll talk more about that too.

Strategy

Strategy is the logic that guides and ties together everything a business does in execution into a value-added whole. The perspective of strategy is a view from the outside-in. Good strategy asks, "How is the world around us changing, and how could we rethink the Back of the Envelope model—and, as a consequence, our execution—to capitalize on that change? How can we build more and better relationships with customers than our competitors?" Strategy involves a continuous questioning of the status quo on the inside and a continual monitoring of what's happening on the outside. It's also a primary responsibility of the person at the top.

The idea of strategy in business also came out of the history of warfare. The earliest principles were borrowed directly from ancient guidelines for capturing hills of advantage, for finding enemies' vulnerabilities, and for exploiting those vulnerabilities in battle. The migration of these ideas into the business world had an explosive effect fifty years ago. A vibrant industry of strategy consulting firms arose to carry these new concepts to the uninitiated.

In its heyday, armies of young consultants, including me, consumed great amounts of clients' funds convolving complex, data-anchored strategies that mesmerized management teams and filled expensive three-inch binders. The universal belief was that the company with the most accurately researched and cleverest strategy would be sure to overcome its rivals and win the spoils in the high-stakes war of business.

Unfortunately, not much of that work really made much of a difference. Most clients felt fine about spending heavily on detailed strategies crafted by outsiders. It was in vogue. But history would prove most organizations incapable of putting the ideas they had paid for into play. Those businesses were too entrenched in their past ways of doing things; the people in charge were too invested in big decisions they'd made previously. The organization was stuck on solutions that had worked in the past. The audience that needed to buy into new ideas in order for new thinking to take hold was too large. As a result, the ivory tower of strategy was seen by middle management and by the rank and file as too far removed from the real world of getting things done to hold much sway. The day after the big strategy off-site meeting and golf tournament, everybody went back to work and did pretty much exactly what he had been doing before.

A little later we'll talk about an approach to strategy that is exactly opposite to this history. Like most things that really make a difference, it can be captured on just a few powerfully thought out pages that everyone can remember and that can be updated easily.

Vision

There are, however, some companies for whom the synchronized evolution of strategy and execution comes easily. But they are rare. Most are run by young people. In these rare organizations, the retoolings of the Back of the Envelope plan and of its execution to match continuously unfolding and insightful strategy seem to happen almost effortlessly. As soon as competitors begin to catch up, these change artists molt and change into something else, leaving their followers roiling in their wake and gasping for air.

Strategy in these companies is not laborious. It doesn't take place at the annual executive off-site meeting. It isn't ponderous. It isn't documented in great detail. And it isn't done by outsiders. Instead, it is spontaneous, cost-free, and occurs at any time and at every tier of the company. And the corresponding adjustments to execution seem to happen almost on their own.

Granted, in no way does the documentation of this kind of strategy and its follow-on execution compare in fit, finish, or academic credibility to the three-inch binders. But, the logic of the new strategy and execution is clear, understood by everyone who needs to know, and continuously improving. When the external environments of these organizations change, a change to strategy follows immediately, sometimes even in anticipation, and employees adapt what they do and how they work almost by themselves.

They are like a large school of fish turning in unison toward food or away from a predator.

I remember being mesmerized by these outliers, and set out in the late 1980s to discover their magic. What allowed a few to accomplish so effortlessly what the others struggled with so mightily and never achieved? I found the answer in a strange place. And finding it was the key that began to unlock for me the mystery of a complete theory of how to run a business.

It was a special kind of vision.

Done well—and most isn't—vision works like leaven to release the inherent potency of strategy and execution. It establishes boundaries for experimentation and emboldens human ingenuity to explore options within those boundaries. A friend taught me to think about this idea as The Theory of Constraints. Constraint yields freedom. When one knows the boundaries of the safe territory, she is far more likely to try new things within those limits. Seeing the edges of the safe territory eliminates fear and releases creative energy.

The concept of vision, which we'll discuss in great detail a little later, was the answer to my question. Vision is the alchemy that transforms execution and strategy from static "limiters" into dynamic "enablers," and that melds the three separate ideas into a super-triptych for running your business. When paired with vision, strategy and execution are multiplied in their individual powers. Linked to strategy and execution, vision becomes the seed for a culture of continuous amazement, success, and satisfaction for everyone involved with your business.

Though I can't yet put a number on the effectiveness gained from using these ideas together, when the phenomenon can be quantified I am confident that the multiplier will be double-digits.

Vision-Strategy-Execution Together

What's so special about deploying these ideas, then holding them in mind, in unison? Where does the multiplier come from? How does a business put them in place and how do they fit together? We'll get to all those questions.

To answer the questions, we'll need to reverse the order of the discussion so far. We'll need to shift from the order in which the components usually come into being, in most instances, to the order in which they should be deployed as the guiding principles for running your business.

Reversed, and moving from left to right, the sequence of Vision-Strategy-Execution becomes the table of contents for the complete story of how to do your job. It is a story that proceeds from big picture to narrow focus. It works from generalities to specifics. It transitions from aspirational to pragmatic. It builds from ideas that stir the soul about the long term to those that direct our hands and our minds every day. It covers the bases of your responsibility. And the opening of this story is the big picture, the general, aspirational, and soul-stirring part: vision.

Chapter 4

The Magic of Vision

My first real understanding of vision unfolded for me in an unlikely way. At about the same time I had become aware of the differences between those rare companies that convolved strategies and operations simultaneous with changes in their markets and industries, versus the majority that didn't, I was also focused on personal fitness and sports performance. Those interests led me to sports psychology.

My doctor told me an extraordinary story about pole-vaulting. He asked me to imagine an aspiration to vault seventeen feet. The likelihood, he went on, of achieving my goal certainly would be enhanced by solid strategy, in the form of a well thought-out training plan. The plan should start with a thorough understanding of my physical mechanics, attributes, and conditioning—this is analogous in business to a definition of the customer. Assuming no obstacles there, the plan should proceed to a detailed regimen of strengthening; training for flexibility, technique, and endurance; rest; and diet—in short, execution. With the training plan in hand, it would be up to me to follow it to the letter.

Then he told me that a superior athlete with strong physical attributes, conscientious execution of a solid training plan, and maniacal focus could expect to clear sixteen feet. But not seventeen. The rare individuals who get over seventeen feet have something in addition. It's not greater dedication to the plan. It's not an extra gene. It's not any factor of heritage, dedication, or environment. And it's not steroids. The answer is vision. The difference that separates the extraordinary athletes who jump over seventeen feet from those who clear sixteen is an ability to place themselves in the moment of their achievement.

A seventeen footer, it turns out, vividly and intensely imagines clearing the bar hundreds of times, maybe even a thousand times, in a day. Involuntarily. He has the ability to close his eyes, feel the spring of the track in the starting position, the oscillation of the pole through his forearms and shoulders as he accelerates down the runway, the jolt at the plant in the box, the flex of the pole, the lift and, finally, the faint brush of the bar at the base of his neck, then the flop into the pit. He sees the scoreboard. He hears the announcer and the roar of the crowd. And he thinks about his mom, whom he wishes more than anything in the world could be there to share the moment. In some way that the pole-vaulter has yet to understand, he knows that she is. All this happens in a microsecond, driven by an overwhelming commitment to accomplish something that is personally important. It happens hundreds of times in a day. Maybe even a thousand.

Since the time of my talk with that doctor, I have been able to see his explanation as a fairly reliable phenomenon in most sports, not just pole-vaulting. In recent years, it has turned into a well-respected principle of therapy and training for performance enhancement. But at the time, I asked, Why not in business? And I could think of no reason.

For a year I obsessed about how vision, as it was beginning to be used in sports psychology, could be applied to businesses. One of the understandings that came to me was that there is much more to achieving the desired effect than simply imagining the result. And I knew that could be the challenge in applying vision meaningfully to business. In addition to being imaginable, the achievement also has to be deeply meaningful, at a personal level, to those who are seeking it. For our pole-vaulter, seventeen feet was not about the medal, the newspaper article, or the roar of the crowd. It was about his dad. Through every day of preparation, all the tough ones when his muscles were sore and when it rained, to the day when he finally cleared the bar, he was measuring up to a set of beliefs and reasons for being that constituted his tribute to his dad.

As I continued to think about the effect of vision on achievement, I became even more convinced that people with the ability to project themselves mentally into an achievement that has soulful and noble meaning have an edge. They have a much greater likelihood of accomplishing something truly extraordinary than those with less noble motivations, like the profit of their division or a promotion.

Vision crafted with meaning yields determined inspiration, both of a conscious and an unconscious sort. Consciously, we will never miss a workout. Unconsciously, we will recognize, and take full advantage of, unplanned, unanticipated, and subtle opportunities to supplement progress that others will miss. And at the moment of truth, we'll bring something to the track that others won't.

So, why not in business?

Eventually the answer emerged. It ran back to the reality of multiple minds in business, versus the one mind of the pole vaulter. First, you must see the vision. But then a whole management team, and ultimately a whole company, needs to feel the brush of the bar and the roar of the crowd—hundreds, if not thousands, of times a day.

Admittedly, this is a tall, tall order. But it can be done. I know because I've done it. Many times. And I am convinced that you have the ability to do the same. I am convinced that there's nothing you can do that will better enhance your business's chances for accomplishing something truly extraordinary than to develop a compelling vision for yourself, and then to infect everyone else around you with it.

Let's talk now about how to do this. In addition to describing an enticing future that engages the aspirations of the workforce, a well-crafted vision also:

Establishes the boundaries of the safe area for employees and, thereby, releases them to contribute all that they might within those limits, and

Establishes the specialness of your organization in the minds of the people you are counting on, which adds an element of pride and a soulful dimension to their commitment.

So, what's the structure, or the architecture, for this kind of vision applied to business? I've found that the most effective construction involves four parts: core values, purpose, mission, and tangible images.

Core Values

The first of the four components of vision is core values. Core values are principles that people want to see reflected in their experiences at work. Sometimes they end up sounding a little like "motherhood and apple pie" but that's okay, as long as the organization lives up to its promise.

Core values describe peoples' aspirations about how they want to live their lives—stuff we're not so accustomed to talking about very often, if at all, in businesses. People are most productive when the values they see playing out at work align with the values by which they aspire to live the rest of their lives.

A business's core values address questions like:

What do we believe in deeply at work?

What principles will we never violate?

What will we attempt to reflect in everything we do—both on the inside and on the outside?

What do we want to stand for?

To what standards will everyone be held accountable—both up and down the chain of command?

In the moments of hardest decisions, where will we look for direction?

All other things being equal, what is it about this company that makes me choose to work here rather than someplace else?

A good list of core values consists of only four to six items. But when chosen and crafted well, these values are timeless. They have to be things that people believe in, and you have to believe them too. If your business has been around for a while, they may turn out to be things that your predecessors believed. And if you do your job well, they are the things that the generations who follow you will believe too.

Where do these values come from? Most of the time, no one has to create or dream them up. They are already there, in the fiber of the business. Maybe they're not acknowledged very often, and they may be a little trampled on; they may have been diminished by abrogation and been left out of nearly all of the "important" discussions about the business for a long time. But in most businesses, the core values are not hard to rediscover. How? By talking to people.

It's not difficult to find out what's on employees' minds here. Often, the values people mention first are those they remember from days past, things that they long to see reestablished in their lives at work. These are things that employees are gratified to talk about with someone whom they believe can make a difference.

I remember starting an informal discussion about core values over lunch with about fifty employees in a 1700-person window manufacturing company, MW Manufacturers, located in the rural southeast. I had recently stepped in to replace the previous CEO and to run the businesss through a transition in strategy, which the owners hoped would improve financial performance and increase the value of the company. The fifty or so employees attending that lunch had all volunteered, and represented a cross-section of the workforce, ranging from a few of the most recent hires on the plant floor, up through the supervisory ranks and middle management, to the CFO.

The previous administration had been low on one-on-one communication, not obviously committed to fairness as a principle, and, while kind and well-intentioned, less conscious about building employees' pride on the footings of personal respect. Once someone had broken the ice on these topics and I had demonstrated that I would respond with interest rather than defensiveness, commentary flowed like water out of a fire hose. Sign-up sheets for the weekly lunches were booked weeks in advance. A purging of sorts was going on.

A little later in this particular meeting, when the torrent of venting had subsided to a trickle, I asked a question: Did our products—residential windows—have any special significance to anyone in the room? There was a silence. For a while I thought people might be having trouble deciding how to respond to such an abstract question from their new CEO. Just as I was about to restate it, a woman I'd not yet met shyly raised her hand. Without making eye contact she lifted her slight frame from her seat and in a soft voice began to tell a story.

Her story was about how she had grown up in a cabin in a back hollow of a neighboring county without running water and without a window. She went on to describe the night after she and her family moved into their first cabin with windows. Through her tears, she told about lying in bed at the age of seven on the first night in her new home and seeing stars through her window. She finished by talking about how this memory would be rekindled for her, sometimes, as she watched our windows track their way through the assembly line. And how she wondered if any of them would be doing the same for another little girl.

Well, I looked around and was more than a little comforted to see that mine were not the only damp eyes in the room. At that instant, everyone present at that week's lunch felt a significance, a responsibility and a nobility associated with our work, that we'd never felt before.

Quickly, then, the first draft of the company's core values spilled out. Over the next few weeks I accelerated the process until I'd involved nearly every employee in the discussion. Each time, people were elated to have a chance to talk about their lives at work this way. And their ideas had an amazing impact on the levels and apparent alignments of their energies. All 17,000 square feet of the plant and offices felt more alive, with everyone talking in small groups about things they'd never considered as part of their lives at work.

The resulting list of core values looked like this:

At MW Manufacturing, We Believe Deeply In:

> *Integrity*
> *Fairness*
> *Respect*
> *Personal performance, and*
> *Products that make a positive difference in people's lives*

At another business, CARSTAR, a four hundred–unit automobile collision repair franchise, the list that arose from a similar procress looked like this:

At CASRTAR, We Believe Deeply in:

> *The nobility of lifetimes of Service*
> *A Family of family businesses*
> *Being Better on every tomorrow than we are on every today*

Purpose

The second part of vision is purpose. A business's purpose sets out, again in the same clear and fundamental language that expresses what it cares about in its core values, why it needs to exist. In fact, the battle cry of purpose often comes out of the same discussions that yield the core values.

When I was in business school, if any professor asked why a business needed to exist and you didn't answer smartly, "To create shareholder wealth," you risked embarrassment and dismissal for the day. There was no questioning of the purpose of any business—the purpose was always the same, to create wealth for its owners—and, consequently, there was no discussion about why any particular business needed to exist. But I think that was wrong, especially for mainstream businesses.

Expect some people who haven't been through a discussion of purpose to be cynical on this point, though they might not show it at first. They might see the notion of purpose as detached from the realities of what they need to get accomplished every day. They may view it as distant from what their supervisor cares about or as overly naive or idealistic when laid against the essential pressures and urgencies of their day-to-day lives at work. And I understand where they are coming from.

One of my clearest observations after more than thirty years of evaluating businesses is that those with a sense of purpose beyond creating profits—those who understand their underlying purpose to be making a contribution to other people or to society—have an energy that businesses focused only on building shareholder wealth can't match. But very few employees, particularly in mainstream businesses, have ever experienced anything other than creating wealth for the business's owners as the central motivation of the people in charge. You can be different. And if you are, your business will improve.

To be clear, I am not making a case against financial performance as a requisite for sustainable businesses, because it is. Nor am I arguing against more earnings as better, because they are. Neither am I arguing that the only good businesses are green. In every business, there are elements that can be seen as doing good for people or society. It's all a matter of what comes first in the minds of the people who are in charge when they think about, and when they talk about, the reason for their business.

There's an often-told story about purpose that serves my point. It's about Johnson & Johnson. If you are old enough, you will remember nearly thirty years ago an episode known as the Tylenol scare. Beginning in the fall of 1982 a news story broke regarding people who had become seriously ill from taking Tylenol. Early indicators pointed to tainted product,

product that might have been tampered with and poisoned. It was just the emergent tip of a huge iceberg, and one that had the potential to stop one of the biggest, most admired, and most profitable businesses in America dead in its tracks.

Johnson & Johnson's Board of Directors held an emergency meeting to decide how to respond to the crisis. The meeting opened with a staccato barrage of analysts' reports on the possible scope of the problem; the likelihood of more attacks; the potential impact on decades of advertising, promotion, and brand building; competitors' likely responses; and the impact the problem might have under different scenarios on the financial performance, stock price, bond ratings, and valuation of the company. The board confronted a dizzying array of considerations with consequences that measured potentially in the billions of dollars.

Midway through the presentations, one of the board members, who had for several minutes been noticeably detached from the torrential flow of information, stood slowly and, interrupting a presentation in progress, asked, "What is the purpose of our company?" There was a long pause, as people adjusted their antennae to an entirely different wavelength. Then a fellow board member responded with the company's mantra, "To preserve and improve the quality of life." Another long moment of silence in shared reflection followed. The analysts' shoulders slumped. Then came the proclamation of the chairperson, "Get it all off the shelves immediately, later we'll figure out the magnitude of the problem and the damage to the company." He was supported with unanimous agreement.

I'm not sure how many companies faced with so potentially devastating a problem could have come to as incisive and, as history would prove, as wise a business decision as did Johnson & Johnson that day. All spurred by a moment's reflection on the purpose of the business, why the company needed to exist.

Few of us will ever face a crisis of the magnitude of the Tylenol scare, but we encounter events from time to time that feel every bit as complex and every bit as threatening to the businesses we run. And in these instances there is nothing I've found that offers more solid grounding and guidance than a clear sense of your business's purpose.

You are not the only one who will function better with a clear sense of purpose. While others in your organization might not encounter problems as thorny as the ones you see, your employees, in the course of trying to contribute their own best work to the company, do run up against situations that feel every bit as weighty and difficult. Like you, they will be grateful to be guided by a clear sense of why the business exists. That understanding, backed-up by clear core values and spread widely, heightens the likelihood that decentralized key decisions will be made in such a way that they reinforce one another and move the company forward in unison.

At MW Manufacturers, the statement of purpose we crafted for the company was:

> *MW Windows exists to improve the quality of life for people in the places where they live.*

At CARSTAR, the collision repair business, the purpose was:

> *To help people through a challenging time in their lives.*

The DNA of Your Business

After working with the idea of vision for a couple of years, I was helping my friend Mike Toth, who runs a very successful and prestigious branding company that focuses on the fashion industry. We were working on a branding and marketing strategy for one of his high-profile clients, a name familiar to everyone, and revered by most. I started telling him about core values and purpose. I could tell he was listening, but also that my words were taking him somewhere else. The somewhere else turned out to be another very important idea. When Mike finally spoke, what he said was, "DNA. Dick, your ideas of core values and purpose, together, feel to me like the DNA—the basic genetic material—of a business, and of a brand."

My mind jumped into overdrive. I knew at that instant Mike and I had hit on a breakthrough: The core values and the purpose of a business are what distinguish it from every other business and mark it, throughout its lifetime, as special. Economies cycle, technology marches on, customer tastes change, and industries come and go, but the DNA of great businesses, regardless of how they evolve over time, stay the same, just as we humans remain the same as we transition from infancy through adolescence to maturity and old age. Sticking with the reality of our DNA gives us the greatest prospects for happiness, for being understood and appreciated by others, and for success over time.

From that day forward, I've always thought about the core values and the purpose of a business as representing its fundamental genetic structure, its DNA, and have taught others to do the same. The results have been hugely satisfying in terms of aligning people with the businesses that fit them, and in providing anchoring guidance to the decisions that move those businesses in the right ways.

Mission

The first two parts of vision—core values and purpose—are concrete and permanent ideas. I'm fond of advising CEOs and company presidents to carve them deep into the granite above the front door. Core values and purpose shouldn't change. They should prevail through different leaderships, business models, and cycles of the economy. Core values and purpose give everyone in the organization some things that they can count on forever. In this regard, they are solid and comforting.

But there's another part of vision, and it's dynamic. It's not the calming confidence we gain from a few important things that we know will always be the same. Rather, it's the adreneline we experience when we decide to make things different, not just by a little, but boldly, and by a lot. It's aspirational, and it articulates for people the next heroic milestone in the journey they will take together in living out the full potential of their DNA. Mission asks, What is the goal employees will dedicate themselves to achieving? What will stir pride? What goal fits iconically under the banner of core values and purpose? This is the mission, the third part of the vision quartet.

There is always a lot of semantic confusion whenever I get to this point and begin to talk to people about mission. "What's the difference between our mission and our goal?" they ask. Or they say, "We've been setting strategic objectives for the past few years. Are those missions?" Because there are so many different uses of the terms mission, goal, target, strategic objective, and the like, I've concluded that it's pointless to try to sort them all out. The only thing I care about is what the concept embodies. I choose to call it mission. If another term sits better with you, feel free to use it.

Great statements of mission walk a knife-edge between what's absurd even to talk about and what just might be achievable through an extraordinary effort. These are the missions that drive heroic outcomes. And these kinds of missions have a far better chance of being realized if they arise clearly and solidly from previously agreed upon commitments to the fundamental canons of the business, from the core values and purpose—from the DNA—of the company. Missions arising from DNA stir a level of passion that is impossible to reach with proclamations that lack this kind of principled anchor. It's especially difficult to reach with proclamations that are only about numbers. And about making someone else rich.

The thrill of setting a noble and heroic goal carries with it not only an infectious sense of adventure and challenge, which comes along with most quests to accomplish something others think isn't possible, but also a more powerful sense of rightness and a sense of duty to a higher calling. These are the kinds of motivations that inspire people to amaze even themselves with what they can accomplish—for example, clearing seventeen feet.

One of the best and most enduring examples of mission that I know was the statement President Kennedy made to Congress in 1961, when he said, "I believe that this nation should commit itself to achieving the goal, before this decade is out, of landing a man on the moon and returning him safely to the earth." That goal qualified as "way out there" in the minds of most Americans at the time. But it was also an exhilarating declaration of mission to a credible group of scientists. Even more importantly, it was a heart-stirring offering of commitment to a country that was overcome with angst about its Cold War with the Soviet Union. Though no statistics exist, my own hunch from conversations with those who were a few years older than I am is that Kennedy's bold statement of mission made a great number of Americans feel proud to be doing their parts for their country in 1961, which was going to be the first to put a man on the moon.

A sage CEO shared with me, from the perspective of his comfortable retirement, what he saw as his most important role in the latter years of his career. His contributions were the greatest, he said, when he thought beyond the limits of everyone else's imagination and picked a goal that was outrageous, yes, but was in line with his and his company's DNA. He would begin talking about the outrageous goal with everyone, not casually but compulsively and relentlessly, until the others started to consider, then to believe, that it might actually be possible. Then it would happen, and he would pick another outrageous goal.

Not too long ago, I picked an audacious goal for a rather tired company that I'd been asked to run as CEO. It was to double production and maintain the size of the workforce. Talk about outrageous! What I did know was that my company, though it was taking in more than $100 million in revenues, had a relatively small share of a huge market. Our doubling of revenues could go largely unnoticed by our competition. Close derivatives of our existing products could provide entry into new market segments. And the lynchpin to making it all happen was to reduce costs: in other words, to dramatically increase labor productivity.

As the mission began to make more sense to me, I started talking about it with a close circle of direct reports. I began with the preamble, "Look, I've been thinking about something that's way out there, but the more I put into it, the more I find myself coming to the conclusion that it just might be a possibility." A few people thought I was nuts, but a few got infected. With the help of the enthusiastic ones, I began to widen the circle. Not too long after that, I began to bring in outsiders to help us think about things that we didn't know enough about, like the landscape of adjacent market segments and the realities of reducing production cycle times, reducing machine down times, and going to full capacity on the third shift in our facility.

Gradually, confidence in the scheme grew and began to spread. When I began to hear others talking about the idea without my provocation, I decided to go public. This didn't mean a big speech with a proclamation, like a political campaign. It was a lot like discovering vision and core values. I began assembling cross-sectional groups from different departments that got to be as large as fifty or so. I began asking these groups what they saw as the major hurdles, not the blocking points, that we would need to get over in order to move in the direction of the audacious goal.

Some people's first responses were reactions to a perceived threat. A goal to double productivity must mean a desire to reduce jobs. No. The second half of the goal conveyed the idea of doubling volume with the same complement of employment. Some still thought I was daffy. But I also began to win many over. And before long, employees in some parts of the business began doing things on their own that they'd decided would test the labor productivity hurdles in their own areas.

Then I stated our mission:

By January of 2000, working together, we shall have doubled our productivity and maintained the size of our workforce.

At CARSTAR the mission was:

By year end 2014, achieve 500 stores in the U.S. and be insurers' first recommendation for their policy holders in the markets we serve.

These missions were clear, measurable, and already believed to be possible by a number of the opinion leaders of the business. People in both companies were excited and for a while came to my office to tell me things, such as:

"I couldn't wait to get home last night to tell my wife and kids what I'm going to be involved in over the next eighteen months."

"Dick, I know that you're going way out on a limb here, but I want you to know that I'm behind you."

"There's a buzz in the plant that I've never felt before."

"Dick, I just wanted you to know that Earl's crew and mine got together at the end of the shift last evening and brainstormed about how we're going to help."

"Dick, I used to think of my operation as an island. Now I am part of something bigger that I believe in and am committed to make happen."

Talk about the rewards of leadership! It was one of those moments you spend a whole career trying to create. In its wake, it leaves you with the greatest sense of responsibility that you will ever feel to a group of people who are not blood relatives.

My job at both companies then shifted from generating ideas to providing direction, resources, encouragement, and recognition for accomplishments that moved us toward the goal. Within reasonable timeframes at both companies, were on the way to meeting our goals—which many had viewed as impossibilities just two years earlier. And we were ready to drive the next audacious mission stakes into the landscapes of our future.

At CARSTAR we had set the foundation for a year of restructuring that led to four years of sequential record-breaking performance and hugely successful recapitalization. And at MW we had set the stage for a rewarding transfer of financial ownership, and for another that would follow that one.

While mission is not the final ingredient in a powerful vision, it is the one that binds the organization together in a spirit of accomplishment and stirs everyone with a sense of pride, along with a motivating dose of angst, for being committed to a noble but challenging cause.

Tangible Images

The fourth part of vision is a much less weighty one. In fact, it's fun. It's where people dream about the lives that they would like to create for themselves, have a chance to talk about it, and finalize their commitments to one another to make it happen. Tangible images are peoples' ideas about the payoffs they might realize when the mission is accomplished. They are their dreams. They are the lists of what individual employees think might be their personal rewards for success.

While the format for the statement of mission is usually along the lines of:

"By (date) we shall have (statement of accomplishment)."

The format for tangible images looks more like this:

"By (same date as mission) my life, by being part of our company, will include (list of desired future images)."

Unfortunately, when most people in charge of running businesses talk about the payoffs for success, they talk only in terms of financial rewards, ones that usually go to someone else. CEOs exhort their constituents to work together as high-performance teams, night and day, harder than they've ever worked before, to increase earnings for the shareholders. Then they are baffled when their eloquence is greeted with the obligatory, limp-wristed applause and vacuous stares. There's nothing in those kinds of messages for the troops. Except, perhaps, the opportunity to keep a job that doesn't mean much more to them than a paycheck anyway!

What about the effects of incentive stock options, or about ESOPs (employee stock option programs)? These are intended to bind everyone together in pursuit of the same thing, higher earnings and valuation, right?

In my experience, few individuals in most mid-tier businesses hold either incentive or ESOP options. Still fewer understand what they are and believe that they will ever pay off. But in the meanwhile, everybody has needs and desires that they care about intensely, and that they can express in very explicit and tangible terms, if we take the time to listen for them.

You learn about your employees needs and desires by using the same process that you used to uncover core values, purpose, and mission. You just talk to people about what moves them: What would be their greatest personal satisfaction if the business accomplishes its mission, stays on the course of its purpose, and lives its core values all along the way? Encourage them to think selfishly. What's in it for them?

Having gotten the other three parts of vision in place, you will find your tangible image discussions truly exhilarating. You're likely to find them surprising too. You'll be amazed at the range of peoples' aspirations, when you gather your first cross-sectional group of employees to talk about their tangible images of success. And you might be shocked at their modesty. When we got to this point at the window company, everyone's top three tangible images narrowed down to:

Job security for contributors and termination for slackers,

A clean place to work, one that they'd be proud for their families to see, and

Stock cars, not on television but just at the local tracks, with the company's name on them.

We didn't have to wait to accomplish our mission to start working on the first two tangible images. They became steps that built important credibility and confidence along the way. By beginning to act on what the employees told us about their aspirations, we uncorked a wellspring of enthusiasm, with an enormous, pent-up hydrologic head behind it. Sure, we might have been able to ferret out those tangible images sooner by skipping over the earlier foundational work. But by taking our time, by building on a credible platform of core values, purpose, and mission, we created an enormous multiplier in the motivational power of the tangible images.

A flood of ideas for improving the business ensued. In short order, the problem was how to sequence and respond to great ideas, not how to think them up. Within twenty-four months, every toolbox in the plant, and most of the bumpers in the parking lot, also carried proudly the logo of a company-sponsored car. Yes, following the cars was a huge payoff. More importantly, the cars—sometimes the winners at the local tracks, though it really didn't matter—were a symbol of pride, pride in what the workforce had accomplished together and pride in being affiliated with the company.

Vision Postscript

The resulting architecture for vision in businesses looks like this, with four parts grouped under two headings:

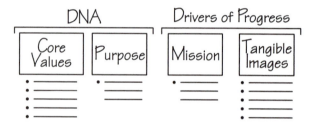

Combining core values, purpose, mission, and tangible images into a cohesive vision installs a rallying point and offers a clear source of consistent guidance on the issues that managers and employees face over the course of an average business day.

The company vision also becomes the first reference point for the big decisions, like:

Who fits into our organization and who doesn't?

What behaviors are acceptable and what aren't?

Which customers and types of business fit us best?

What kinds of policies and procedures are appropriate in our business?

What do we say about our business when talking about it to others?

What do we do when things don't work out as planned?

How do we handle crises?

As each of the four components of your vision takes form in your mind, you may be surprised to find them coming into play involuntarily, when you are wrestling with the big questions. Your core values will begin to affect how you think about your options. Your purpose will further narrow your choices. Your mission will inspire you in choosing one that, perhaps, is tougher than the others. And your tangible images will sustain your energies through the rough spots that often follow.

But a big multiplier on the effectiveness of your time takes over as soon as all four pieces are in place, and as soon as other people begin to see the logic of the whole story. A new appreciation for what they are striving to accomplish together arises, as well as an understanding of why the goals of your company are important and the benefits that they will enjoy once they reach their goals. Vision gives higher meaning to everyone's life at work and, therefore, greatly enhances the likelihood that the company will accomplish something extraordinary.

It also simplifies your life:

Once an employee checks alternatives for a major decision through the screen of vision, at least half of their choices fall away. What's left over will include some selections that are better than others, but generally most of what's left will be okay.

When people at every level of your organization see their decisions against the same background, the likelihood is higher that their individual actions will complement one another. And they'll take complementary actions without oversight, because all their decisions are guided by the same vision.

Companies with a strong vision have the right people doing the right things—with more energy and creativity and with less oversight and waste—more often than their rivals. But a solid vision also becomes the platform for an entirely new, more efficient, and more effective approach to business strategy.

Built on the platform of vision, strategy can become a simpler exercise, more incisive and easier for an entire organization to understand and commit to achieving. It's something that is easier to adjust, in real time, in order to maintain synchronization with changes in the business environment.

Chapter 5

Converting Vision into Reality: Strategy and Execution

Crafting vision, by itself, is sometimes an inspiring exercise, but also much less impactful in organizations than it could be. Sometimes it's even damaging. Why set expectations that never will be met? Why associate yourself with proclamations that everyone else knows are unrealistic? Why set standards that will never be enforced? All of these outcomes undermine your credibility and sap confidence in your organization. So, my advice is: Don't embark on vision unless you are committed to following through.

But there is always risk in great vision. Great vision, through the statement of mission, "walks the knife-edge between what's absurd to talk about and what just might be doable." So, how do you assure that once you open the topic, you end up on the "doable" versus the "absurd" side of the resulting prescription?

The answer lies in the crafting of the second and third elements of the Vision–Strategy–Execution model. And it lies in continuously cycling back through the entire three-part logic as it's coming together to test and to refine the integrity and reasonableness of the entire story.

Strategy That Counts

Strategy, the next part of the Vision–Strategy–Execution framework, has come a long way from newly minted MBAs presenting costly findings to big company CEOs. But truly effective strategy has yet to find its way into most mainstream businesses. Everyone talks about it, many do it, but few get as much out of it as they put in. Strategy is still something that's usually done once a year, off-site, and generally in the fall as a preamble and a trial balloon for budgeting.

Most mainstream businesses that do strategy have stopped spending on expensive outsiders. They've figured out how to do it for themselves. They've found ways to make the research part less resource intensive and the documentation more concise, and there is also growing appreciation for involving more people in the exercise. But there is still something missing from the ideal of strategy: Good strategy is the battle plan that guides "visioned" businesses to timely and effective execution of their missions. Built upon the platform of vision, good strategy and its subsequent execution accomplish the mission and deliver the tangible images defined in the business's vision. That is the ideal.

But the sad fact is that while many managements still view strategy as an important ritual in running their businesses, few attribute the successes of their businesses to the strategy process.

It's not that people haven't tried. Books have been written and read, tracking models have been developed, and seminars have been run that attempt to tie strategy to meaningful achievement through things like compensation incentives, balanced score cards, and peer reviews. The very need for these books and seminars makes the point that strategy isn't yet central to the creation of value in most mainstream businesses. It's still extracurricular and peripheral, one step removed from the way people actually spend their time at work every day. Yet, it endures and remains a key responsibility of most mainstream CEOs, who reset the strategy every fall and then try to figure out how to get others to pay attention to it.

Strategy is like church for some people: It's a responsibility they are reluctant to ignore and try to take care of on Sundays. But the sermon recedes in their thinking for the rest of the week. This approach to strategy doesn't make much sense.

The preamble of vision lays the groundwork for a better alternative. With vision as the backdrop, the approach to strategy can be entirely reconceptualized. Built upon the platform of vision, crafting and maintaining strategy becomes less time consuming, more continuous, more relevant, and more effective as a tool for running your business and delivering results.

This new idea of strategy is everything that the old idea isn't:

New	Old
Practical	Theoretical
Tied to execution	Abstract
Relevant range	Long range
Concise	Detailed
Decentralized	Centralized
Spontaneous	Programmatic
Participatory	Exclusive
Flexible	Rigid
Fast	Slow
Free	Expensive
Moving target	Set game plan

Why does a solid vision make this kind of strategy easier? Because vision binds an organization together at important conceptual and emotional levels and prepares the business for, even creates anticipation for, the discussion of strategy. Through vision, employees understand more clearly how the organization thinks about the future. They have had a chance to contribute to the company's guiding principles, and they have had the opportunity to decide for themselves whether the intended outcomes match what they want. When the fit is good, employees are enthusiastic about participating in strategy in order to make their vision a reality. The social cohesion that the vision process brings to the company paves the way for a new style of simple, powerful strategy.

So, how do we shift the discussion away from the conceptual ideas of vision toward new thinking about defining pragmatic and effective strategies? The direct link from vision to strategy, and the starting point for the discussion of strategy, is the third of the four big ideas that make up vision: the mission. A well-crafted mission narrows the focus of strategy. Under your leadership, that focus can be directed assiduously to rest on those major things that stand in the way of accomplishing your mission within your agreed timeframe. The need to honor, through lengthy conversation and documentation, everything that everyone is involved in—a common flaw in many strategy processes—goes away. The resulting list of core initiatives that the company should commit to forms the main part of the strategy; in addition, the document should provide brief explanations of why each strategy is important and how it will get done. Include, too, everything the company must maintain under its current concept of operations. The strategy should be able to be documented on no more than three pages. That's it!

Regarding whose ideas get included and whose get left out of your strategy document, you do indeed want everyone to come out of the strategy process feeling important. But the truth is that most things that consume resources and that occur on a day-to-day or month-to-month basis have little strategic significance. They maintain the current Back of the Envelope model for the business, and they cloud the discussion of strategy. The point of your strategy discussion might well turn out to be that you should change some of those things.

Over the years I've sat through hundreds of strategy sessions and processes that start out as unbounded information scavenger hunts for the "hidden clues" for success. These sessions also may involve a sub-rosa agenda of justifying every key manager's current activities. The trove of irrelevant findings is so great that the real clues—the things that could drive the business to its next tier of accomplishment—remain hidden. Another unhelpful approach drapes a thin veil of credibility over an executive's predetermined ideas about the route to success. Both are wastes of everybody's time.

An open-minded pooling of knowledge and perspectives to surface the few things that stand between you and the achievement of your mission is the most useful exercise. Billed this way, and following a team's participation in the creation of vision, it's usually not very complicated. Most management teams who have been around their businesses more than a few years have both the competence and the understanding they need to contribute to adequate strategy. This is particularly true when the teams are brought together around shared emotional principles and aspirations.

The notion of "adequate" as a qualifier for strategy is important here. Because drafting a strategy that's inarguably superior to all others is not the goal of an effective strategy process. This is different from the way many people think about strategy. Yes, the original idea behind strategy was that the company with the best one would win, at the expense of its competitors. After a lot of trials and a lot of money spent on consultants, however, the conclusion is, that's just not right.

The key to a business's success is usually not in the absolute superiority of its strategy. Most businesses can select from a number of strategies, any one of which carries a reasonable potential for success. So the right approach is not to argue to death the merits of each to find the very best one. That's time consuming and divisive. And by the time the dust has settled, circumstances are likely to have changed and it's time to start all over again. The trick is to be fast. Pick the strategy that makes sense to most of the people who will have to execute it. Begin its execution. Be quick to monitor the results along the way, and be expedient in refining the strategy based on emerging findings. The line that I'm fond of dropping on this topic is that, "The third- or fourth-best strategy executed superbly well usually wins."

So, what does this shorthand approach to strategy actually look like? How does it compare with conventional thinking and practice? Where is it different? Where is it the same? And how do you get at the promises of improved economy and effectiveness from doing it?

Think of your strategy as today's "game plan" for getting from where you are right now—your current reality as expressed in your legacy Back of the Envelope model—to where you want to be—the accomplishment of your mission. State the strategy as simply as possible, ideally on fewer than three full pages, consisting mostly of bullet points.

Where does this game plan come from? The best strategies come from the people you will be counting on to execute them. Strategy is multidimensional in ways that most other aspects of running your business, and many of your people, aren't. Which means you need a multidimensional group to formulate it.

My preference for the first rounds of strategy discussion is to involve the leaders from each functional area of the business. As you and this team begin to zero in on strategy options—say, a list of six to ten possibilities that would require significant support from the functional areas—ask these functional area leaders, your initial strategy discussion partners, to engage their key reports in follow-on discussions and to report their findings back to the group.

But isn't there usually some rare "genius" who creates great strategy? Doesn't it arise from a unique and clever idea built around someone's unusual ability to see things that others can't? I don't think so. I've seen too many perfectly effective strategies emerge organically from the collective understanding of an existing management team for me to believe that strategy requires unique genius. I've seen too many successes to be persuaded that the same potential doesn't exist in nearly every mainstream company in America. As a counterpoint, I've also watched an awful lot of strategies developed by "big head" outsiders fail miserably.

So, what is your role in this approach to strategy development? First, emphasize your intention to build a strategy that moves you explicitly toward your vision. Second, emphasize your intention to encourage your team to think freely about how to move your business from its current reality to its mission. Let them know that you will be looking together for the four to six big things that will enable your business to deal with the big issues and opportunities it faces in its market and competitive environments and, thereby, to move quickly toward your stated mission.

In addition to assembling your people to think together about big strategies and conditioning them to build that thinking on the platform of your vision, there is another important role for you, or for someone under your direction, in facilitating the resulting conversations. This is to separate strategies—the big ideas that match the big issues and opportunities in your business environment—from tactics—the subtasks or steps that a wide circle of employees, including you, might do in order to execute each strategy.

Because many managers see the world of their businesses most clearly from the perspectives of their own jobs, they are understandably inclined to bring their own pet issues to the discussion with the hope of sponsoring them as strategies for the entire organization. In the context of your whole business, these "issues" may in fact be tactics that may or may not support a higher level strategic initiative. It becomes your job, therefore, to keep the discussion at the higher level of strategy, matching everyone's thinking to the big, core issues of your business.

So, what are the clues that can help you recognize the differences between strategies and the tactics that may or may not support them? And how do you keep positive momentum while leaving some people's pet ideas behind? It's really not all that difficult. It's a matter of using what I call "nested thinking," a form of compartmentalizing or segmenting these into distinct components.

There is an overpowering tendency for people in meetings to get "captured into" the topic of discussion. It's why so many well-intended meetings turn out to be pointless. The topics aren't controlled, but wander off into irrelevant territories, and everyone follows. Meetings are particularly susceptible to this type of wandering when the agenda for discussion is as vague, and subject to individual interpretation, as it often is when defining strategies for a business.

Your job here is to stand on a level that is different from the rest of your team. Building from the platform of vision that you, collectively, have established, and from the mission you have stated, your job is to continually ask yourself, "Is what is being discussed directly related to achieving our mission?" And if so, "Is what is being discussed the best articulation of what needs to be done, or is it a subset of things we might consider doing to achieve a higher outcome?"

In a process I really can't explain, the right set of initiatives, articulated at the right level, will emerge for you if you maintain this focused posture in overseeing your team's discussions of strategy. The big parts of the puzzle, your strategies for how your business gets from where it is today—your current reality—to where you want it to be—your mission—will arise from the discussion and will begin to take form in your mind. As they do, with an appropriate dose of humility and respect for your team, you can begin shaping the continuing discussion to add further clarity for your own understanding, and, concurrently, to shape their thinking to align with your own. I know that this sounds like manipulation. And it is. But it's okay. Because your job in formulating strategy for your business is, first, to listen to and process all the data from your team against the backdrop of your vision, and then to align everyone's thinking around the few high-level things that need to get done in order to move you from your current reality to your mission. Undirected thinking of groups isn't good at this kind of convergence. You need to be. And when you are, your strategies will emerge.

So, what does the architecture for the discussion that leads to clear and incisive strategy look like? It begins with a critical look at the current reality of your business from three perspectives—your market, your industry, and your own competitive positioning. Through this three-part evaluation, the core issues facing your business will arise. Then strategies are set to deal with the core issues. The overarching structure for your discussion of strategy looks like this:

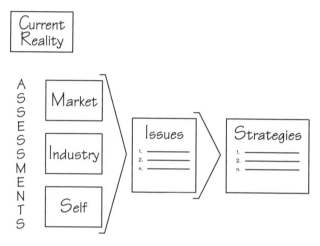

Before launching into the first of the three assessments that constitute your current reality, we'll look at a couple of definitions for terms that people often confuse. I use *market* to mean the entire universe of people who buy things and the dynamics that influence their decisions. *Relevant market* means the same thing, but is narrowed to include only the people who buy, or could buy, the things you supply. I use the term *industry* to refer to the "sell" side of the buy–sell equation, the opposite of the market. *Your industry* is the universe of companies that provide things that could satisfy the same needs your own offerings do; it's essential to be aware of the dynamics that are occurring within this population of suppliers. Your self-asessment, then, summarizes how well you stack up against your rivals in capitalizing on the current conditions and trends in your market and in your industry.

Current Reality—Market Assessment

Most businesses have a pretty good sense of what's going on in their marketplace. This is because they deal with their customers daily. In lots of businesses, however, this sense isn't compiled in a very useful format. Typically, it's piecemeal, with different parts residing in different people's heads, with varying degrees of currency and with varying breadths of perspective. It's often all there, somewhere, but it's not assembled cohesively or accessibly. At least once a year, therefore, you should consolidate this wisdom, record it succinctly, and share it.

In the early fall, I often circulate a memo to my management team and to others I think are knowledgeable about customers and about demand; in the memo I call for their wisdom on our market. My note alerts these key individuals that in a few weeks, as part of our strategy discussions, we'll be meeting to reconfirm our collective understanding of the conditions and dynamics of our market, and it asks them for their thoughts in advance. It includes a checklist that I want everyone to fill out and return to me so that I can consolidate the results before we assemble.

At the beginning of the memo, I restate my own understanding of our vision and our Back of the Envelope theory of our business, highlighting the scope of what I characterize as our relevant market. This is a direct "take off" from the message of our mission, the third part of our vision. If, for example, our mission is to become the leading supplier of high-end, residential roofing materials in a five-state region of the Southeast, we don't need to know much about demand trends in the Dakotas, or nationally, for that matter, unless we believe that there might be trends emerging there that will become significant to the high-end residential roofing business in our five-state region. Nor do we need to know about the demand for low-end residential or commercial roofing. They're not in our relevant market.

Building, then, upon the definition of our relevant market, I ask each participant to answer the following questions. Shorthand bullet-point answers are best. You don't want to require people to write lengthy prose. And you don't want to have to wade through it all.

Relevant Market Size and Growth

How big is our relevant market and what rate of growth—units and dollars—do we expect our market to experience over the next year? Over the next three years?

Pricing

Do we expect pricing to go up, down, or to stay the same in our relevant market over the next year? By how much? Over the next three years?

Segmentation

Within our relevant market are there segments that are defined by differences in what's required to make the sale (like products, price points, terms, service, etc.)? What's required for selling into new construction, for example, might be very different from what's required to sell into replacement roofing situations. How do the segments compare in terms of size, growth, and pricing?

Channels of Distribution

Are there different channels of distribution for getting our product to end users? Or are the distributors our customers? What's required to be successful in doing business with the different channels? Looking forward, do we see some channels gaining over others? How do the channels compare in terms of size, growth, and pricing?

Trends

Are there any other significant trends that we see taking place or affecting our business in our relevant market? For example, are we seeing smaller houses, more attention to roof aesthetics, or new building codes, and how will these affect the roofing materials business in our relevant market?

Basis of the Buy

Looking at everything we know about our relevant market, what factors do we believe will have the greatest impact on the purchasing decisions of customers we want to be doing business with over the next year? Using a scale of 1 to 5, how would you rank the significance of each factor? For example:

Basis of the Buy at XYZ Roofing:

Price	5
Product Performance	5
Personal Selling	4
Service Level	4
New Products	3
Community Image	3
Promotion	3
Advertising	2

The management teams of most businesses have enough perspective to answer these kinds of questions with a level of understanding that constitutes an acceptable description of the current reality in their market. The thinking that it provokes also may uncover new insights about opportunities or threats, such as an opportunity for a new product or changing tastes that may make your current offerings obsolete. Without such a strategy exercise, these opportunities and dangers might go unattended.

Current Reality—Industry Assessment

While assessment of the market is all about customers and demand, the industry assessment is about your competitors and about the dynamics though which you vie with one another for business. Though most businesses have enough understanding of their industry to "talk a good game," my continual finding is that companies' understandings of their industries are far less accurate than their understandings of their markets. And I think I know why. It's because we deal on a direct basis with our competitors far less often than we deal with our customers. Direct intercepts with our rivals are relatively infrequent, and they seldom reach the level of intimacy we often reach in understanding what makes our customers "tick." Plus, it's self-justifying, self-satisfying, and just easier to discount, or even to demonize, our competition as stupid or nefarious. The result is that our understanding of our competitors is almost always far less current and far less accurate than our understanding of our customers.

Accordingly, I've been astounded on more than a few occasions by how inaccurate many management teams' assessments of their industries and their competitors are. I see so many businesses "blindsided," even mortally wounded, by a "dumb" competitor's "unexpected" move that could have been predicted and countered—if anyone had been paying attention.

So, attached to the same memo that I circulate in the fall—the call for wisdom on the market—I also issue a call for wisdom on the industry. The same guidelines apply. Everyone submits bullet-point responses to the Industry Assessment Checklist by a date early enough for me to compile the results before we meet face to face. My Industry Assessment Checklist generally includes the following questions.

Industry Size and Growth

How big is our industry—both in the number of players doing what we do and in dollar volume? By how much do we see it growing or declining over the next year? Over the next three years?

Structure and Share Distributions

The structure of most industries takes the form of a hierarchy of participants, which can be characterized as residing at different tiers:

Dominant Players

Everyone else must respond to the competitive moves of a dominant rival in order to remain viable. (Note: there are no dominant players in many industries.)

Strong Players

Not strategically threatened by another rival, and with maneuvering room of their own.

Tenable Players

Followers, at risk of being targeted by strong or dominant players.

Weak Players

Survive only due to the lack of interest in their businesses on the parts of more powerful players, including, perhaps, our own company.

Make a list of our key competitors and rate each one as dominant, strong, tenable, or weak, noting the shares they control of our relevant market and the trajectories of their growth.

Game Plans

Michael Porter, in his seminal work on competition, narrowed all of business strategy down to just three options, or strategic positionings: low cost, differentiation, or focus. Optimizing on one may suffice to sustain a business for a while, but combinations are better:

Low Cost

A position of endurance and high strategic leverage based upon the ability to satisfy customers' needs at a lower cost than competitors.

Differentiation

A position derived from being different and better than all your competition at some aspect of the business that is meaningful to customers.

Focus

A position derived and sustained by aligning your business better than any other competitor to the unique and meaningful needs of a specific market segment.

Characterize each of our key competitors' game plans according to Porter's options for strategic positioning.

Key Competitor Profiles

Make a bullet-point list of what you think stands behind each of our key competitors' strategic positioning.

Make a list of competitors' advantages we should consider focusing on how to draw their customers.

Outlook on Share Positions, Pricing, and Margins

Given all of the above, what do you think is likely to happen to share positions, pricing, and margins in our industry, including our own, over the next year? Over the next three years?

Current Reality—Self-Assessment

The last piece of the puzzle in your company's current reality is strategic positioning. Every time I go through this assessment with a company, I continue to be impressed by the effect that prior open and honest thinking about market and industry has on people's abilities to understand more accurately the realities of their own strategic situation. That is, compared with what they would be carrying around in their heads otherwise. It's natural to delay taking the time to think rigorously about the big picture of our businesses. We all have a tendency to put it off. It's your job not to let that happen.

Stephen Covey, author of best-selling books on business and leadership, talked about this avoidance flaw as our preference for the "critical" over the "important, but not critical." It's so much easier to fill our time at work attending to critical things, whether they're important or not. How many times have you gotten to the end of the day and thought, "Wow, where did that one go?" or "I really didn't get anything done today that I'd planned, but I'm absolutely worn out!" You're not alone. But neither are you exonerated.

We all find that responding to things that are brought to us is less demanding than figuring out for ourselves how best to use our time. Furthermore, it's fairly common to be reluctant to examine ourselves too closely. We tend not to look because of our fears of what we might find. For these reasons, self-assessment isn't something that most of us look forward to or go out of our way to do very often, or very well.

Unless you are willing to stand by, observe, and accept whatever comes to your business as the result of changes in your marketplace, and as the result of your competitors' actions against you, someone's got to ensure attention to these kinds of questions in your business. Not doing so is like night sailing with neither compass nor radar; it may be okay for the moment, though probably a little unnerving, but it's highly likely to get you into unthinkable trouble eventually. If you're the person running your boat, the someone who attends to the company's strategic positioning ought to be you.

So strike while the iron is hot! After my managers have completed their bullet-point assessments on the market and the industry, I ask them, while they're still in the mood, to complete one final list—one that evaluates our own business. The Self-Assessment Checklist, which I attach as the final item in the fall mailing, includes the following information and asks the following questions:

Past Performance (I provide basic information for the most recent twelve months and for the past three years on the form—revenues, gross margin dollars, earnings, capital consumed, return on investment)

How do you view our performance—financial and nonfinancial—versus our plans over the past year? Over the past three years?

Baseline Performance Outlook

If we continue on our current track without significant change, what will our performance—revenues, gross margin dollars, earnings, requirements for capital investment, return on invested capital—be next year? What will it be three years out?

Competitive Positioning (Here, I provide a chart for them to fill out to rank our company against our key competitors according to the elements of the "Basis of the Buy" and to note for me any other factors that they might see as relevant)

How do you see us stacking up against our rivals?

Basis of the Buy

	Price	Quality	Service	Convenience
Competitor "A"	—	—	—	—
Competitor "B"	—	—	—	—
Your Business	—	—	—	—
Competitor "C"	—	—	—	—
Competitor "D"	—	—	—	—

Rate competitors versus Your Business:
5. A Lot Better
4. Better
3. Same
2. Worse
1. A Lot Worse

Market Positioning

How do we stack up versus trends you have identified in our market? How are we seen by our customers?

Organizational Strengths and Weaknesses

Keeping in mind our statement of mission—the third part of our vision—make a bullet-point list of what you see as our organizational strengths and weaknesses.

Strategy Strengths and Weaknesses

Keeping in mind our statement of mission, make a bullet-point list of what you see as the strengths and weaknesses of our current strategy (I provide a list of what I see as the key elements of our current strategy here).

Taken together, this summation of the market assessments, industry assessments, and self-assessments constitute the current reality of your business. There should be no need for anyone to devote more than two pages, bullet points only, to each assessment. One page is better. That's three-to-six pages, total, that detail each person's take on the current reality.

Sorting Out the Big Issues

When I receive everyone's inputs, I assemble the whole collection in a loose-leaf binder and read it several times with some reflection time in between the readings. Then, I begin consolidating, eliminating the overlap, which is usually considerable, and highlighting the differences. It usually takes me a couple of hours a day, over two to four days, to digest the material and create the consolidated report, which I return to each contributor, along with the material he had submitted and a cover letter. In that cover letter I let each participant know:

> That I appreciate his input.
>
> That my consolidation is simply a "first cut" at compiling everyone's input—not my own version—and that I expect the final results that we will create together could be quite different.
>
> That we will be meeting to accomplish that end.
>
> And that at that same meeting we will be identifying the issues, from our updated understanding of our current reality, that we need to deal with in order to move together toward our mission.

I usually schedule three half-day sessions to review my takes on each of the three topics, with a few days between each session. The advance distribution of my highlights from everyone's lists, coupled with the employees' own experiences in working through the questions, has the effect of setting good boundaries for the discussions. I seldom have to intervene, except to ask a key question, summarize points as they are made, and move things along. With this preparation and intention, the meetings usually take on lives of their own. The sessions are wide open and serve to consolidate everyone's thinking and to update the current reality of the business—through assessing the market, the industry, and current positioning within the boundaries I've set. And the meetings usually go remarkably well.

One of the other things I've learned after nearly two decades of doing this is that it's impossible for a group of informed managers to talk about the current reality of their business, against the backdrop of their mission, without also thinking in specific terms about what needs to change in order to open the way for achievement of their aspirations.

At the end of the three sessions two important things have risen to the surface. The first is a fresh shared perspective on the current reality of the business, to which a lot of people have contributed. Second is the list of the big issues that I've been looking for—the major things that have to change in order to open a path to achieving our company's mission—along with the support of the team behind them for getting them done.

I usually wind up these sessions on current reality with another, explicit discussion to confirm the key issues of our business—the things that, if we attend to them well, will move us along at an acceptable pace toward our mission. In the event this discussion reveals that the issues involve things that are clearly beyond our capabilites to solve, we need to go back, respecify our mission, and proceed from that point. That would be an unfortunate finding, but it is one that's unlikely, particuarly if you've involved knowledgeable people along the way. Even if that's what happens, it's still preferable to committing youself to a set of outcomes that you'll never achieve. Napoleon learned a lot about this principle in Russia.

Formulating Business Strategies

Strategies, then, are a set of simple but powerful statements of what your business will commit to do—in addition to what you're already doing to run your business as it exists today—in order to redirect it toward achieving your mission. There's usually a one-to-one relationship between the big issues that arise from your discussions about your current reality and your list of strategies; for each big issue that you need to resolve in order to accomplish your mission, you will need to formulate a strategy. It's not uncommon, however, that the strategy you choose to solve one issue has a "spillover effect" on other issues. In fact, it's great when this happens—it means that you can employ a smaller number of strategies to address a larger number of issues.

Following is an example of an issue that arose from a market assessment, together with the strategy developed to resolve the issue:

Issue #1:

Mergers among many of our more significant customers will result in greater buyer leverage and demands for more competitive pricing over the next two years.

Strategy #1:

Institute global sourcing and productivity improvement program to reduce cost of goods sold by ten percentage points within eighteen months, net of program costs.

Another issue from the same company and its corresponding strategy, this time from the industry assessment, was:

Issue #2:

While we enjoy significant excess capacity, the earnings of a number of our tenable competitors are declining, threatening their existence over the next two to five years.

Strategy #2:

Through accretive mergers and acquisitions, consolidate tenable players' business into our manufacturing and distribution infrastructure constituting a 25 percent increase in revenue and a 30 percent increase in gross margin dollars within twenty-four months.

And still another example from the self-assessment portion of the exercise was:

Issue #3:

Our current compensation schedule is being bettered by new industries moving into our region, which is jeopardizing our workforce.

Strategy #3:

Institute aggressive training and gain-share programs for employees, with a target increase in compensation of 20 percent, with program and compensation cost increases offset by gains in productivity, within eighteen months (an example of "spill-over benefits" with Issue #1).

Exceptional Execution

Once a strategic plan is in place, execution commits resources to, and builds assurances into, the *operations plan* and the *budget,* for the accomplishment of your individual strategies.

The science of management has given us a lot of great tools for doing this: Gantt charts, critical path analyses, linear programs, and others are relevant. The ones I find most useful are simply the operations plan and the budget. However, I've found confusion in many organizations about the differences between the operations plan and the budget. The existence of a strategic plan helps to clarify the roles of these two tools, which can be seen as the second and third steps, respectively, along a continuum of specificity that runs from the general to the more specific. That continuum begins with the strategic plan. And it ends with the operations plan, which specifies who is going to do what, when, in order to deliver the strategies. The budget then summarizes the specifics of what the plan is going to cost, what the financial results are expected to be, and when the results will be delivered.

The Operations Plan

While your strategic plan outlines what your entire business intends to accomplish and how, your operations plan describes, at a finer level of detail, what each unit of your organization is going to contribute to that outcome.

Once the strategic plan has been drafted, I join each member of the original team in presenting it to the people who report to her. Then we ask each of them to create an analog story for her own area of responsibility, applying the same collaborative method we used before. Against the backdrop of what we are planning to accomplish together as an enterprise—our strategic plan—I ask them what they will do, in their own areas of responsibility, to support that effort and the achievement of our collective mission.

For instance, continuing the example on page 60, Strategy #3 is a commitment to aggressive training and gain-share programs for employees with a target of increasing compensation by 20 percent. As his input to the operations plan, the Human Resources Department leader must detail what he is going to need and what his department is going to do to accomplish those outcomes. As with the strategic plan, I also want rough order-of-magnitude estimates from all the managers of the costs, timing, and benefits of their responses.

Almost never do the first drafts of the resulting submittals add up to something that makes sense. It's not because the people running the lower operating units of the organization aren't smart, or because they don't care enough. In fact, it's just the opposite. Because they are inspired by the vision, and because they know their units' roles and believe so greatly in their potential to contribute to the strategic plan, they often see roles for their groups that are beyond the means of the company to support.

So, I usually count on two things happening here. One is having my own eyes opened to things that I hadn't been able to visualize before. The other is that I'll recognize a need to rein in some of the zeal that the combination of the vision and the strategic plan has released. Also, my review of the submittals almost always reveals interesting interrelationships among the strategies and new insights about what the different units of the organization might be able to contribute that the higher-level team and I had not fully recognized before.

As a result, I expect to have a discussion with each author about her submittal in order to (1) better understand the thinking behind the proposal, (2) bring expectations into closer alignment with the realities of the available resources and the results that will be required, and (3) explore further the interrelatedness of what different people will be doing to support the same ends.

The resulting compendium of these outlooks—the ideas from the different units of the business about how each can contribute to accomplishing the portfolio of strategies that make up the strategic plan—constitutes the operations plan. And, following the same model that we used to define the strategies, I gather together all the contributors to the operations plan, present my compilation, and ask for their commentary.

Once we've settled on the operations plan, which is usually no more than three to five pages of bullet points and a chart that indicates who we are counting on to do what, when, it's time to test the reality of the scheme through budgeting.

The Budget

Everyone running a business or even thinking about it should be familiar with a budgeting process of one sort or another. Most simply, budgeting is an exercise of projecting the future performance of the business, taking into account the experiences of its past. A budget must also account for differences expected in the future due to changes in the market and industry environments and to the company's introduction of new strategies.

In usual practice, the budget starts with a summary of financial performance in P&L format over a recent accounting period. The management team then uses what it's learned since the last budgeting process to adjust the numbers going forward. The discovery of a new product or a new market, for example, might have promising prospects for increased sales. Similarly, adjustments in material prices or adjustments in plant operations might portend different product costs.

Budgeting is not too different from the process used to arrive at the vision, the portfolio of strategies, and the operating plan, except in one regard. The budget consolidates the effects of the strategies and the operating plan into a financial outlook for the business in such a way that you can see the impacts of the individual initiatives. The approach I find most useful, and most insightful, is to make the initial pass at the budget as if the strategic plan and the operating plan didn't exist. What will performance be like in the absence of anything "strategic," if we keep doing pretty much the same things that we've been doing over the past year? I call this the "baseline" outlook. The next step is to "layer" the financial implications of the strategies and the operating plan into the baseline outlook and to observe the effects.

Most strategies and operating plan elements will have costs and benefits associated with them that are relatively obvious, and that can be estimated at a level of accuracy sufficient for this kind of budgeting. As an illustration, Strategy #1, from our earlier example, was to:

> *Institute global sourcing and productivity improvement programs
> to reduce cost of goods sold by ten percentage points within eighteen
> months, net of program costs.*

Introducing the two programs will have costs. Those costs associated with global sourcing will likely be best reflected as a new line item in the purchasing subsection of the general and administrative costs category of your budget, labeled something like "Strategy I—Global Sourcing." The costs associated with productivity improvement will likely be best "layered into" the manufacturing overhead section of your cost of goods sold and labeled similarly.

Together, these two initiatives are expected to yield a net reduction in the cost of goods sold by 10 percent within eighteen months. This is a little more complicated, but not by much. First, as is the case with most strategies, the positive effects don't appear on day one, but rather build up over time. The budgeting team, therefore, needs to forecast this buildup of the expected effect and spread it over the strategy's implementation period. Second, while the overall result will be a reduction of cost of goods sold, the effects can likely be traced to reductions in raw material costs and a reduction in labor, both subcategories of cost of goods sold. These can be shown, again as new line items "layered into" the baseline outlook, either separately at the levels of material costs and labor—which is preferable—or combined for a less-detailed tool for tracking results in a general offset to costs of goods sold.

In its final form, the budget looks a lot like the outlook, with the important exception of several new line items—both costs and benefits—that correspond to the strategies and include the effects of the operating plan. These new line items should increase significantly the likelihood of the company's survival and improve the projected financial performance of the company.

Execution Postscript

Through an operations plan and a budget anchored in, and emanating from, solid vision and strategy, businesses optimize their available resources and channel them to accomplish their strategies, to move toward their misssion, and to optimize their financial results.

As an important additional benefit of operating plans and budgets that arise from shared and concise understandings of vision and strategy, companies react more quickly and more effectively to unanticipated changes in the circumstances of their businesses. In so doing, they put even more distance between themselves and their less well-run competitors.

People love to be a part of businesses like these, businesses where the employees work together to fend off challenges by making advances rather than playing defense. These are places where change is not avoided but greatly anticipated. The resulting esprit de corps, loyalties, and commitments to one another are unrivalled. In the next section we'll examine the underlying concept for building this spirit of confidence, of adventure, and of winning into your business.

Chapter 6

The Theory of Renewal

In the late 1960s, Bruce Henderson, founder of the Boston Consulting Group, offered a theory for the evolution of businesses in his celebrated discussion of the product life cycle. It has been an anchor point for business thinking ever since. Henderson postulated that businesses, like biological organisms, track inevitably through a four-part life cycle.

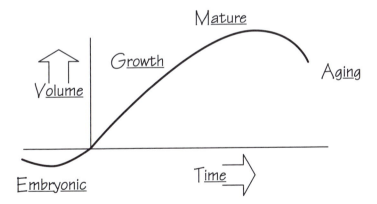

Of the millions of ideas for new businesses every year, only a very few make it out of what Henderson called the embryonic, or concept and development, stage. Like frog eggs, where only one in a thousand or so ever emerges as a tadpole, most new business ideas never get past the drawing board, either outside or inside existing enterprises. Of the tadpoles, only a few are lucky enough to make it to infant frog-hood. And of those few that emerge as infant frogs, still fewer make it to adolescence, in our case to a minimum level of sustainable business revenues that cover costs.

Of those enterprises that achieve stability as embryonic businesses, another one in a thousand or so will have hit upon a truly powerful business model—one that survives the Back of the Envelope modeling process and that actually has access to the resources needed to execute it. These few will have the chance to transition from the embryonic stage into growth organisms.

At the point of transition into the growth stage, the senior tadpole business emerges as a raw freshman into a new and more competitive world of grown-up frogs. All are competing for the same bugs and the same spots on the best lily pads. In order to survive, the young frog must transform quickly into a vigorous aggressor, competing competently and fiercely for all the elements required for his survival. Soon he learns that safety can be found only in continuous growth and improvement. As friend and author Chris Crowley points out in his book *Younger Next Year*, biological organisims have only two settings: betterment or deterioration. Stasis is not an option. Businesses in the growth stage are like that, too.

Beyond the growth stage, Henderson argued that all organisms, and business concepts too, begin to slow down and settle into a subsequent stage he called maturity. And I agree. In businesses, the shift to maturity occurs when new technologies arise to displace old ones, pipelines of demand are satisfied, hoards of competitors emulate the success of the growth-stage pioneers, or buyers' tastes simply change.

Beyond maturity Henderson predicted inevitable aging and decline.

Extending the "Natural Law" of the Life Cycle

Bruce Henderson's idea was genius. His business-as-organism analogy was one that people understood instinctively from the very first time they saw it. In its clear, graphic representation they saw a way of simplifying a business principle that they'd always suspected existed, but never quite had a way of isolating as a concept so they could talk about it.

In 1974, I was one of those people fascinated with Henderson's observations. But the more I thought about the business life cycle, the more it bothered me. And I thought about it not over a period of weeks, but over several years. What bothered me most was that, while in many instances the life cycle explained exactly what I saw going on, I also knew about exceptions. There were businesses that didn't seem to mature, age, wither, and then die over time. Somehow these businesses found a way to defy the fundamental law of existence.

Some of these death-defying businesses were the same ones I had noted as the almost effortless change artists when it came to new strategies and associated execution. And it was these companies that had truly intrigued me by continuously leaving their rivals behind them, stupefied and stuck in the later stages of Henderson's life cycle and losing ground as time claimed its victims.

The first and most obvious examples of these life cycle anomalies were in science and technology–related industries, those dealing with computers, software, medical devices, or consumer electronics. But then it began occurring in other industries, like fashion, where the pace of changes in taste are fast. In each of these industries, there was a handful of companies of scale that seemed to have the capacity for continuously staying ahead of the pack and preventing their followers from launching any serious challenges. These businesses had something that transcended natural law. In these organizations, as one business model transitioned from growth to maturity, another model surfaced. Apple Computer, Microsoft, Boston Scientific, Sony, and Ralph Lauren were, and still are, emblematic of this phenomenon.

As I looked further, I found examples that suggested that the secret was more than a matter of leadership in scale. A smaller German performance car company, for instance, migrated successfully into the luxury class, and eventually had one of its cars cited by both *Consumer Reports*—for value—and *Road and Track*—for performance—as the best in the world. A Seattle coffee shop's brand became ubiquitous, at the same time setting new price and taste standards for a cup o' joe. A regional airline demonstrated new concepts in service and a cost structure that reset economy travelers' expectations and which launched it from a brash upstart into the envied model for US carriers of the future. And there were more.

The point is that none of these businesses accepted the inevitability of the life cycle of their business model. Nor were they all of one ilk. These possibilities seemed to be available to nearly any business that had the will to identify timely strategic alternatives and to move away from their old patterns and begin fitting themselves to new ones.

With these findings, a variation of Henderson's concept began to take form in my head. The most admirable businesses, it seemed to me, were the ones that had found a way to develop a culture that intentionally foreshortened their own life cycles, shedding their fears of the unknown, convolving and demonstrating ever more relevant business concepts over time.

The energy in businesses that operated that way seemed addictive. But unfortunately, the prospect of that sort of change is also monumentally daunting, particularly for those of us conditioned to a different rhythm and way of thinking about business dynamics. It would also be daunting to imagine one's own organization learning to be comfortable and confident with a future in which our business model might be short-lived and continuously shifting.

There is a way to make this transition, but it is available only to those businesses that see their worlds through the tri-focal lenses of Vision–Strategy–Execution. And it looks like this: It is the concept of renewal, whereby one curve isn't the whole ballgame for a business. Rather, one change leads to another, and to another, and so on.

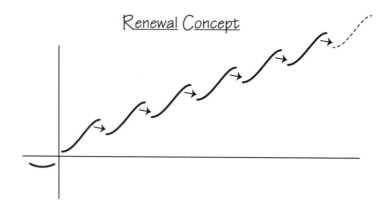

Renewal, versus stasis, is the core model for existence in companies like Microsoft and Ralph Lauren. These companies see as their overarching principle of operations the idea of defying the "natural law" of the life cycle. They accomplish their continued renewal by redefining their Back of the Envelope framework and their aspirations about mission and tangible images as quickly as they can. You can do it, too.

Defying the Curve

It was in these life cycle–defying businesses that I saw the first examples of how renewal-based businesses operate. They were continually seeking to change what they had worked so hard to put together in the past. In these businesses there is no intellectual rest. Everyone rides a wave of energy that comes from being vested with responsibility for ingenuity and performance. It is like the responsibility a master craftsman feels for the unexcelled beauty and utility of the things he produces. His aim is to make every outcome better than his last.

There are no anonymous humans in these kinds of companies. New ideas come from everywhere and are valued, whatever their source. Experimentation is encouraged. It occurs, however, within agreed-upon boundaries and according to a set of shared understandings: first, about the core values and purpose of the business; second, about the mission and the tangible images it strives to accomplish; and third, about the strategy and execution plan that everyone understands as the path for getting to the goal.

When widely and deeply understood, these underpinnings of the culture raise the odds that individuals' efforts will build upon and complement one another and that they will raise the readiness of the collective whole to move forward boldly and in step, rather than in conflict. The company can act as a team, in synchronization with what it needs to do in order to stay aligned with changes in its environment, to the betterment of itself and its customers rather than its rivals and their customers.

Structure and rules aren't primary in these organizations. They're secondary to, and derive from, clear and collective understandings of what needs to get done and, generally, how it needs to be accomplished. This is not to say that life in one of these forward-thinking organizations is unstructured or easy. It's not. It's just that the pressures are different. However, for the right kinds of people—those interested in growth in their own lives through their experiences at work—the rewards are far greater.

So, how do these kinds of businesses defy the inevitability of the life cycle? The answer is that they don't. Rather, they transition from old life cycles onto new ones as quickly as the old ones wane.

Below is what I call the Cross Renewal Model. Let's examine the renewal model diagram and see how it works.

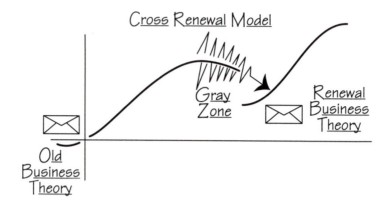

Note, first, that the jumping off point from the old life cycle curve to the starting point on a new one occurs well before the growth stage of the old curve starts to flatten out. This is a tough order. How, for example, do you convince a management team to think about doing something new and different when business is going so well? And why would you want them to?

The answer lies in the power of imagination. Left to our own devices, most of us don't use our imaginations very well. We continue doing what's most comfortable most of the time. Remember the story of the poached frog who doesn't notice that the cold water is getting warmer and then hotter until it's finally cooked? It is easy to miss changes that happen slowly over extended periods of time. What compels those who do it better than most of us is an ability to dream up something even more enticing than our current preoccupations—an ability that I believe almost everyone has—coupled with the encouragement to pursue those dreams—which is something a lot of us don't have, particularly at work. Henry Ford once said that he wished when he hired employees that he only got their hands and not their minds. You need a very different attitude.

Note also that the route from the old life cycle curve to the new one is not a straight line. In fact, it oscillates wildly. The amplitude of the swings is greatest at the outset, like a radar homing in on a signal; then it begins to narrow as the distance to the target shortens. There's an analogy here with sailing. Say you need to traverse to a point on the other side of the lake in moderate fog without a compass. You set an initial course in what you know to be generally the right direction. After a while, you tack to a setting roughly ninety degrees off your previous heading. A little while later you reverse the process. A little while later, you change once again. You zigzag across the lake in your general direction until you are close enough to see your mark, for which you then set your final course.

Transitioning to the Gray Zone is like that. You can't wait until you can see your destination on the opposite shore before you get started. If you wait for that, you will never begin. Rather, you must find the resolve to try something that you doubt will get you all the way to where you want to be, but that you know will get you closer. Once that's done, and with the knowledge you've gained on your first tack, you repeat the process, and you continue doing this until you pick up your mark and can set a direct heading.

This is not the precision stuff of the science of management from the 60s. It's more like intentional trial and error. But when it is impossible to chart a failsafe course at the outset, it's the best you can do. What makes it a better or worse experience has a lot to do with having the wisdom to decide when to change tack and the courage to swing the tiller.

Jumping the gap between two curves is never a predictable path. Nor will it conform to the best of your intentions with regard to timing. The instincts and moves with which you've grown comfortable can become traps. Plans are good exercises in thinking, but they generally don't work out. Lay across the tracks. Bet your career. And you still will not be able to make the transit occur according to plan. That's why I call it the Gray Zone.

Next, notice that the starting point on the new curve is at a point lower than the jumping off point from the old one. I didn't draw the renewal diagram that way by accident. As much as most owners and managements, particularly in publicly traded companies, hate to admit it, seldom will a business transition into a new life cycle and maintain its level of performance from the old one. There are temporary costs for continuous evolution. This explains why there are so many poached frogs, why so many businesses mature, age, and fail rather than renew. Many businesses are afraid to risk a step backward for the prospect of taking greater steps forward, greater steps achievable only by taking the risk to transition through the Gray Zone to a new curve.

Finally, note that a new Back of the Envelope model lies at the foot of the new curve. Renewal is about redefining your business in meaningful and fundamental ways. It's not tweaking around the edges. And you really haven't done it until you can re-specify your previous Back of the Envelope model in at least one of its four dimensions: your customers, their needs, your positioning versus your competitors', or your competencies. And when you redefine one dimension, you will find that adjustments to a few of the others usually follow. Things that don't change the model in significant ways are best thought of as "tweaks," or as variations on the existing business model, rather than as new ideas that trigger renewal. Great companies don't confuse the two. Always strive for the latter.

So much for the logic. Now we come to the question of how, in actionable terms, you transform yourself and your team into the kind of organization that thrives on the idea of renewal. It involves a role for you that might be different from the way you have operated in your company in the past. This role entails being the catalyst that provokes the best thinking from the entire organization, and brings it together into an internally consistent and strategically sensible story for your business. You are the "head learner," which is a lot different from the "command and control answer man" that many of us imprinted on in the earlier years of our business careers.

Chapter 7

Building a Culture of Learning from One Another

So far, we've talked a lot about the logic and the structure of the Back of the Envelope and Vision-Strategy-Execution frameworks. And we have talked a lot about renewal as the core concept for a vibrant and enduring business. We've also talked, in general terms, about some guidelines for installing these ideas in your organization; I've told you, for example, that you won't be able to do it all yourself, it's going to take some time, and you may have never done this kind of thing before, but you are capable. Let's talk now in more specific terms about how you can get to your goal of nurturing a culture of participation and renewal.

Learning from Your Team

How does a CEO, a president, a department head, or a project team leader actually get these ideas and this new style of thinking, in fact the seeds of a new culture, deeply embedded, not only in her own mind but in the minds of her entire staff. How can they be embedded in such a way that the exercise is more than just an annual "going through the motions" routine, after which people go back to doing their jobs pretty much the same way they did before. How can the ideas be integrated in a way that they become part of everyone's conscious and unconscious ways of thinking about the business, and about their own roles in the business? These are healthy questions to ask yourself, and, while every business situation is a little different, there is some very reliable and fungible experience to build upon to get your own thinking, and then the mindset of your entire team, tracking on a new path.

The story that I like to tell people interested in doing this for themselves is about a beautiful old wooden speedboat. In my mind's eye, she's a construction from the 1920s or 30s, the kind of boat you might have seen on a lake in New England or on Tahoe: racy, low to the water, perilously narrow for her length, with two or three low windshields set before red leather–trimmed cockpits, separated by varnished decks. She sits dockside like a piece of fine furniture, glistening with a finish that looks a foot deep, offset with nickel hardware, the patina of which speaks volumes about her heritage. How is she kept in such an extraordinary state of repair?

Well, it wasn't always the case for this particular boat. Her current owner rescued her from a local yard just two years ago in a state of cosmetic freefall. She'd been stored outside without proper cover. Shards of varnish lifted from her rub rails. The hull planks exposed by exfoliation were mildewed black in streaks. Her decks were a pocked field of milky bubbles and burst blisters.

The new owner spent the first four weekends at the new boatyard with an assortment of scraping devices and bloody knuckles. The initial work was hugely exciting, like an archeologist unwrapping a mummy, revealing the underlying details, the beauty, and the flaws of the treasure from the sarcophagus, a small section at a time. But soon, when the enormity of the task became more evident, the work turned long, hard, and painful. Progress felt excruciatingly slow, and inched along at an agonizing pace up to the midpoint. Only after the midpoint of the unwrapping part of the project was an image of the result appreciable enough to inspire him to the finish.

Finally peeled of her beggar's clothing, the boat stood again nobly in her nakedness. Her raw mahogany exuded an aroma that only added to the imagery of what might be forthcoming. Next followed a period of two weeks' rest that was fortunately accompanied by dry weather, to ensure that moisture trapped deep over the decades had the chance to escape. Then followed a thorough sanding and a potent and stinging bleach wash to strike the remaining mildew. The seventh week was one of low humidity, and by the start of the eighth weekend, the speedboat was strikingly admirable in her most honest, unadorned condition. No one had seen her like this in more than sixty years. Closer inspection revealed a few spots where the grain had lifted from the bleach, and these were quickly cut back down with fine-grit sandpaper. Then came the first coat of clear varnish. At over a hundred dollars a gallon, it spread like liquid silk beneath the rakish angle of a sable brush.

After just two and a half hours, she glowed. Those hours, in contrast to the hours spent scraping, flew by, and the piquant aroma of the varnish that filled the shed was intoxicating. But, turning away, the owner left, knowing he had to allow the first coat to cure before he could return the next weekend to apply another. When he returned, he gave her a light rubbing with steel wool and a once-over with a tack cloth to collect the dust. Then he applied the second coat of varnish. And she looked even better. He was still a long way from the foot-deep mirror coat he imagined, but the boat looked remarkably better.

After another four weekends, with curing times in between coats of varnish, it happened. Whammo! With the seventh coat, the entire surface exploded magically in its depth and luster. Two more weeks of sealing and curing, and she would be ready for the installation of the refinished hardware, the interior fittings, bottom paint, and launch.

Establishing effective thinking about vision, strategy, and execution in a business is a lot like creating the "whammo" finish on an old wooden boat. It's not the product of one grueling three-day planning session at the annual company retreat. I've tried it that way too many times, and have come away convinced that it just doesn't work. And worst of all, having invested so much in those kinds of efforts, many managements haven't the heart to admit their disappointment, and they move forward under false pretenses about the quality of their commitments.

Just like work on the boat, there is a natural pace to progress in organizational thinking that can't be accelerated. And now, after nearly thirty years of helping companies build their businesses, I am convinced that the simmering time is every bit as important as the active attention. Aristotle wrote about this phenomenon, and later classical scholars coined it the "Eureka Phenomenon." According to scholars' accounts, Aristotle would focus relentless attention on a problem or on an idea for a while, then retire to a hot bath. There, he would completely unburden his mind from its prior occupation. After a while, the answer he'd striven to find would come to him, seemingly out of the blue. Maybe in the tub, or maybe on a casual walk. Eureka! And that's the way it has worked for me in business organizations. Every time.

Understanding this timing of revelation is the anchor point for establishing expectations that are honest and accurate at the outset. There's nothing more demoralizing for people than getting all keyed up to deal with something that, first, is important to them, and, second, has been a source of serious concern for quite some time, and then failing to get it done. In the worst cases, the best of intentions get tarred as naïve and a waste of time. In the better scenarios, the participants are polite, but after the retreat they return to whatever they were doing in pretty much the same way they'd been doing it before, only less motivated.

A New Role for You

If the de rigueur annual retreat led by an outsider is ineffective, then doesn't that mean that the responsiblity for initiating and leading this whole process falls to you? And isn't it true that what's exactly right for one business won't be exactly right for another?

The answer in both instances is yes. But the comforting news is that the key elements of your role—the ones that get you to an acceptable outcome in nearly all cases—seem to be pretty much the same. Whether you are a new appointee or a veteran in a public or private business, or even in a nonprofit, the basic guidelines given here apply to you. If you follow these guidelines, your efforts have a high likelihood of being productive. The precise details of how you proceed will make your result just a little bit better or a little bit worse the first few times. But on these finer points, take comfort that you'll get better with every round.

What if your business and your management style are informal, and you find yourself a little uncomfortable being "presidential?" You're not unusual. First, believe that from time to time your team wants you to be presidential. This is one of those times. And second, know that if you follow the advice that comes next, you will succeed.

Starting with an agenda for your first discussions with your team on vision, strategy, and execution, I've found, is usually the wrong thing to do. The purpose of your initial gathering with your team on every new topic should be limited to finding out what's on their minds, and shouldn't be a grandstand for letting them know what's on yours. That comes later.

Tips for Being the Learning Catalyst for Your Team

Asking people what they think in front of a lot of other people is usually not the best way to find out what's really on their minds. This is particularly true when people perceive that the territory for a discussion is risky: that there might be factions that disagree; that the issues are complicated; or when the stakes are high. A private setting for your initial discussions about the current state and future of the business is almost always better for getting new ideas rolling.

Having private discussions, and taking notes about each of the participants' ideas and concerns, as a preamble to the first gathering accomplishes a lot of things. It conveys to each person that you really are interested in what he has to say. It lets him know that his ideas are important to you. With the questions you ask and with the way you ask them, you can communicate that you are open to others' contributions shaping your own thoughts. And it affords you the opportunity to test ideas as they are formulating in your own mind. There are few things that have more motivational impact than a superior who is comfortable enough to share her own questions about the business, and to share her emerging thoughts with her reports and to ask them what they think.

Along a different line, one-on-one conversations as a prelude to a group discussion on a new topic also allow the leader of the process to begin conditioning the participants to the boundaries and to the level of discussion that she hopes will follow. This gives everyone the time really to think about and prepare to take an active role in the first gathering.

Before launching the entire Back of the Envelope and subsequent Vision–Strategy–Execution exercises in a new company, I usually schedule as many back-to-back days as it takes to spend at least an hour and a half with each participant, at least a week before the first gathering. I take fifteen- to thirty-minute breaks between the sessions and record my insights along the way. After six or so back-to-back interviews over a nine- or ten-hour day, I'll lose at least a few good thoughts by the end if I don't record them as they come to me.

Once the initial round of individual discussions is complete, I pore over my notes. Usually, I read the entire record at least a half a dozen times. On the first pass I just read. For the next pass I underline, circle, and add additional insights in pencil. On the next pass, I underline, circle, and add more notes in red pencil. For the next I use blue ink, then red ink, then bold black. Finally, I synopsize the key observations and ideas, being careful to disguise any that might be so obvious as to reveal their source.

It may sound odd, but in every case the layering-on of my edits has the effect, not of confusing the record, but of simplifying it in such a way that the most important observations somehow rise mysteriously from the multicolored mess of pages. And when they do, I have complete confidence in the results.

For me, it's important to get all this done within a few days after the initial interviews. Otherwise, it takes too long to get myself back into the moment, and I miss things. When my first draft of findings is complete, I invite all the participants to schedule a second one-on-one discussion if they'd like. I've found that many people think of things that they wish they'd said just after our session ends, and they appreciate the chance to get them in.

My script for each of the discussions follows pretty much the same pattern. First, I outline the Back of the Envelope model for describing businesses and then describe the Vision–Strategy–Execution model and draw the pictures. I also draw the renewal curves with the Gray Zone in between. This part usually takes about fifteen minutes and I set it up with an opening paragraph that sounds something like this:

> I'm glad we've got this opportunity to talk. I'd like to begin by sharing with you a couple of frameworks that I've been using recently to think about our business.

> Then I'd appreciate spending the rest of our time together really listening to your thoughts along these lines. This will be of great help to me in preparing for an upcoming gathering that I have in mind as a vehicle for pooling all of our best thinking about the future of our business.

> For this to be an effective use of our time, this needs to be a candid, no-holds-barred discussion. And in that regard, I commit to you my full and unqualified confidentiality regarding what we'll be talking about, and I'd appreciate the same from you.

Once I've gotten through my introduction and the pictures, I simply ask the person if what I've been talking about makes sense to him. Nobody ever says no, but that kind of transition allows me to shift the controls to him, and allows him to take the discussion in whatever direction interests him most. From that point on, I just listen, ask qualifying questions, restate things that he's said that seem significant to me, and direct the conversation as necessary to cover all parts of the model. I'm careful to avoid the temptation to reveal my own thinking, because I don't want to bias his. And if we run out of time before we hit all the bases, that's okay.

Some of the phrases that I like to use in moving the dialogue along are:

> I've really never thought about what you've just said that way. Could you give me a little more of the background to your perspective?

> Help me understand if I'm making the right connections here. When you said "W" and then later said "Y," it leads me to conclude "Z." Is this the way that you think about it?

With whom do you have these kinds of one-on-one discussions, and who do you consider including in the subsequent process? I generally include all of my direct reports, and allow them to nominate other candidates. The rules of thumb I've found most comfortable are:

> Include no more than a dozen people; six or fewer is better.

> Don't involve anyone who has authority issues. People who'll be conditioning what they say according to who will be hearing it will waste everyone's time.

> Avoid "grandstanders." Some people have a need to be heard, over and over. Either don't invite them, or make them aware of their tendency and your lack of appreciation for it in advance.

> Include and encourage well-grounded differing opinions. I heard a long time ago that the role of the person in charge is to encourage, then intervene among everyone's passionate pursuit of what she thinks is right for the business.

And finally, keep your own thinking out of the dialogue. These conversations are about your staffers' thoughts, not yours. Your role is to be the catalyst rather than the answer giver.

Initializing Your Cabal

Your intent in assembling your team is to forge a sort of modified cabal. The dictionary defines cabal as "a small group of secret plotters, as against a government or authority." And that's exactly what you want, with a couple of important qualifiers. First, every member participates at your discretion. Participation is not a right, and this is not a democratic process. As easily as one can be included, he can be dismissed. The people you choose need to see this appointment as a sign of your confidence in their abilities to think selflessly and constructively about the business. And they need to see it as a privilege to be asked. Second, the authority to be plotted against is not you, but rather current thinking about the business. The plotting is not reckless. This group needs to convene around you to offer different ways of seeing things and to deliberate over them, according to the Vision–Strategy–Execution framework.

With the background of the one-on-one discussions you've had with each member, the cabal can come together for its first meeting in a different way from the annual golf and strategy outing. Everyone knows the purpose and the framework for working together, and has had ample time to think about how she is going to participate. Nonetheless, an advance document is helpful. In the transmittal I send to team members before our first gathering, I usually thank everyone for spending time with me, recall briefly the Back of the Envelope and Vision–Strategy–Execution frameworks, outline a few of the particularly interesting themes from the one-on-ones, and provide an agenda.

Regarding the schedules for meetings like this, I've done it in many different ways: back-to-back all-day sessions (the worst); an all-day session with a half day following (better); and an afternooon, then a working dinner, with a recap the following morning (best). I've also conducted them as a relatively unknown newcomer, as a familiar veteran, and as an outsider. One of the things that holds true across this entire matrix of circumstances is that most people's effective concentration runs thin after about four hours of sitting in a room together. Even to get to hour four, the pace needs to be pretty brisk. What I've taken from my experience is the following:

> If you need more than half a day together—and you will—spread it over two days. Use the afternoon of the first day, and the morning of the second.

Take frequent breaks.

Get everyone involved. Ask questions, don't preach. Short, ten- to fifteen-minute breakouts with teams reporting back to the group help.

Homework helps. Give out an assignment before assembling and ask each participant to report her findings briefly. It's okay to do this at the end of the first day for reports, and on the second day, as well.

Adjourn the first afternoon a couple of hours before reassembling for drinks and dinner together.

Set an example and turn in early. Don't be tempted to be "one of the rounders" at the bar.

Start the second day by asking the group what ideas or observations might have come to them overnight.

Don't worry too much about finishing. The point is starting. Any group that gets through the whole Vision–Strategy–Execution discussion in less than about thirty hours together hasn't done a very good job. Remember the wooden boat story and the value of "curing" time.

At the end of one session, construct the agenda together for the next gathering, set a date, and make assignments for individual members to bring back perspectives on the "holes" in the existing knowledge base you might have uncovered through your discussion.

Should you hire a facilitator or not? My preference is always for management teams to lead this process themselves. And that's part of the point of this book. But there are times when an objective outsider can be helpful. This is particularly so when (1) the critical issues facing the business might be outside the wheelhouse of most people's areas of experience, like a new style of competition or dramatically changing circumstances in the marketplace, (2) the critical issues have to do with friction or questions of competency or fit among the senior team, or (3) you need an outsider's credibility to present a provocative argument, such as the likely impact of changing technology, procurement practices, acquisition activities, or regulation that "shakes" your team into considering new ways of thinking about the business.

A skilled facilitator can ask the tough and insightful questions that will help you and your team navigate these troubled waters. Businesses also find third parties helpful when the opportunity for the future lies in a fundamental rethinking of what the business has been about up to that point. It takes a special perspective and set of skills to maneuver through this territory when those inside the company may be too married to, or mired in, the status quo to lead a dramatic rethinking and possible reorientation of the business on their own.

Whether your sessions are facilitated or run by management, try to get a synopsis of each meeting out within three business days of its adjournment. In addition to summarizing the discussion, you should take the opportunity in the memo to let everyone know whether you think the process is going well, to recognize key contributors to the last meeting, to restate main ideas that emerged, to identify things that should be done better, and to lay out the yet-to-be-resolved items and assignments for your next gathering.

How many gatherings will it take? It depends on the congruity of your group, their degree of understanding of your business, and the complexity of the situation your business is facing. Usually, I find that after three to four sessions, with simmering time in between, the story starts coming together, enthusiasm builds, and it's time to go on.

Spreading the Story

Once the plans for the business begin to gel, the story needs to become part of how each employee thinks about and performs his job. This means asking each member of the original cabal to share the story with his own business group. They should then ask each of their reports, in turn, to continue to cascade the story downward until every individual in the business has had a chance to put his imprint on the result.

What about dissent or additional ideas that emerge in the cascading? Ask that all of this feedback be passed back up the line—e-mail notes are fine—to you and the original participants. Your timely and thoughtful responses can convert these follow-on inputs into powerful "touchpoints," whereby their contributors experience the opportunity to add their imprint and thereby, become avid "owners," believers, sponsors, and supporters of the final product.

So, coordinate with each member of the originating cabal to respond to every one of the new ideas and matters of dissent. Thank each contributor for his insight, and then explain either how the insight has added something important to the story or why it is not entirely appropriate at the current time, but greatly appreciated nonetheless. It's a lot of work at the outset, but with your refinement through each subsequent round, it gets easier.

At this point, you will be on your way to accomplishing two important goals. One is establishing a new and pervasive framework that employees use, both consciously and unconsciously, to think about your business—on their own and in their groups. It is a truly rewarding moment when you find your employees talking excitedly among themselves about the business according to the framework that has emerged from this process. The other goal you are approaching is a much greater willingness for you, your management team, and your other employees to consider ways of changing past practices—of renewing the business—by stepping away from your long-established and hard-won comfort zones to take full advantage of what you now understand as the reality of your future. Paraphrased from a favorite author, Mary Baker Eddy, you will have found the courage to leave false landmarks, and joy to see them disappear.

You are striving in your organization to achieve a mindset where the principles of the Back of the Envelope and Vision–Strategy–Execution frameworks and the Cross Renewal Concept spur a culture of action, of optimism, and of creativity that grow out of a spirit of learning together. And once the mindset is established, you will have put in place the platform for a more simple, a more reliable, a more efficient, and a more inspiring approach to leadership and management.

Chapter 8

Demystifying Leadership and Management

It's difficult to go through a day at work without hearing someone talking about leadership or management. We use the terms to differentiate good companies from bad. We also attribute successes and failures to performance in these areas. And everyone agrees that excellence in these skills is a cornerstone for an effective career running businesses.

But judging from the way I hear the terms often used, I don't think that most people have a clear understanding of the differences between the two. And it's hard to become really good at something when you don't quite know what it is.

As with many other business topics, a lot has been written about management and leadership. But the Vision–Strategy–Execution Model constitutes the most cogent framework I have ever seen for understanding not only the differences between the two, but how to succeed at both as well.

Leadership

Thirty years ago, when I was training to become a naval officer, I was given a course on leadership. Mostly, it was about how to present yourself and how to preserve your status as a leader in a system where the number of stripes on your shoulder determined your authority. We studied the "bearing" of an officer. This meant how you looked, who you talked to and who you didn't, what you talked about with whom, and how you disciplined others. Leadership in the U.S. Navy was about fulfilling the responsibilities of the position that the government had given you. And there are some valuable insights to be gained from this perspective. What I never understood from those years, however, was the idea of a universally applicable prescription, or a handbook, for leadership. It seemed to me that leadership was more about who you are than about how you wear your clothes, how you address your troops, your physical posture, and whether you follow the rules.

By the late seventies, the seeds of a different approach to leadership were beginning to break ground. This, I believe, was an entirely predictable response to the entry of generally better-informed people into the workforce, people who had been taught in the sixties to question authority, to demand their rights, and to be suspicious of the people in charge. The shift in thinking brought about by the social changes of the 1960s rewrote the rules for anyone who aspires to stand in front of others as a leader. True authority is not granted today by position or by statute. Rather, authority is bestowed by those who agree to be led. Today, leadership is not about achieving position. It is about creating followership.

But blind followership is not enough. Effective leadership creates a following that is committed to more than doing what they are told. Effective leadership means creating effective support. The difference between followers and supporters is this: Followers follow because they don't have a better alternative, while supporters support because they believe in both the cause and their leader. They believe that their cause is just and worth fighting for. And they believe that their leader shares, and moreover embodies, the values that they hold most dear, and which they aspire to exhibit in their own lives.

A theme throughout this work so far has been adaptation: Adapt or, eventually, cease to exist. The most effective leadership of a business, therefore, is that which initiates and fosters the most effective adaptation. But as we've noted, adaptation is change, and change is seen by most people as risky. There's no way around it. So, why would a mid- or lower-tier employee risk change and its consequences? Only because of a burning belief that things might be bettered if he takes the risk, because he feels a margin of safety in doing so, and because he feels supported in the endeavor by the company's authority figure. It's the creation and maintenance of those circumstances that I call leadership.

A lot has been written about leadership recently. The best of the current thinking is that leadership is less a matter of personality or presence, and more a matter of one's ability to hold in mind and deal credibly with two different perspectives:

First, an accurate reading of the current situation.

> I believe this links back to a smarter and more informed popula-
> tion of employees in most businesses today, who know for them-
> selves something of the realities faced by their companies, and
> who want to be reassured that their leadership is aware of the
> same. Not talking about the elephant in the room breeds distrust,
> and it's far better for today's leader to acknowledge the reality
> of the circumstances, no matter how discouraging, and ask for
> support rather than attempt any form of shielding or deception.
> Trust is hard won and easily lost, and in today's environment
> this virtue is difficult to maintain with anything less than full
> disclosure. As a comforting corollary, I've often been amazed at
> the good ideas that I've gotten from others as a result of living
> according to this rule. When trusted with a candid disclosure
> of the circumstances of the business, people come up with some
> remarkable ideas.

And second, a picture of something that could be better.

> A number of years ago I was embroiled as the CEO in a business
> that seemed hopeless. Every time we'd get one life-threatening
> problem behind us, we'd uncover two more. Without denying the
> criticality of the moment, I found myself retreating frequently
> to my imagination, where I had created a vivid picture of what I
> had once believed this company could become. I found that talk-
> ing about it with others gave them the same respite that it offered
> me. Then I remembered counsel I'd been given years before by a
> retired CEO who, in reflecting on his career, opined that his great-
> est contributions had been to continue to, as he put it, "advance
> the ball." Leaning heavily on the enticing picture he'd painted for
> himself of what "could be," he avoided becoming overwhelmed by
> obstacles and, thereby, buoyed everyone else's courage by simply
> putting his head down and not giving up in just "advancing the
> ball."

What the Vision–Strategy–Execution Model contributes to this thinking is a conceptual backdrop and a set of tools that afford almost anyone a better chance of chinning the leadership bar than he might have otherwise. I know this because I've seen it work. I've used it myself and have seen it work for many others as well, many of whom wouldn't be among most people's picks as strong prospects for leadership.

On the diagram, the bar above the far left and left side of the center circles indicates that vision and the first parts of strategy are the components for effective leadership. Think back in history. Has there ever been an effective leader who has not had a compelling vision and a theory of strategy that helps people see a desirable future and believe in its possibility? I don't know of one. Vision and the logic of a believable strategy help people think beyond the limits of their own experiences. They anchor great courage. And they offer a language that allows people to reinforce one another in maintaining their commitments and their confidence in the cause.

What we've added below is a title for the arrow that makes the connection between vision and strategy. It's called inspiration. Free people choose for themselves to follow one leader versus another because they are inspired. Those who come to work for more than a paycheck, who strive to do their best, and who stay longer than they have to do it because they are inspired.

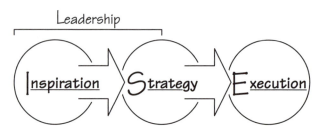

I've often asked people to think about the days when they've driven to work champing at the bit to get there, versus the days when they've dreaded the end of the trip. Their answer is always that on the good trips, they are inspired by something that they expect to be a part of that day. How many days are like that for most people? Why not all of them?

The balance of good days and bad days depends largely on the quality of the company's leadership. And your ability to provide good leadership depends on whether you have the capacity to make your team feel like they are part of a vision at work that resonates with the way they want to live their lives, and whether they are inspired by the story you tell them about how they can make it a reality.

A leader without vision and without a compelling and believable story of strategy is an empty suit. People recognize that immediately. And nothing is less motivating than having to serve a leader who has no credibility. Nothing makes the drive to work more agonizing.

An Overview of Management

A huge body of literature has been amassed over the last two centuries on the topic of management. Today, there's a book on every aspect of management that you might imagine, with additions being made to the library daily. For me, the easiest way to think about the topic is to break it up into four parts, each of which corresponds to a different focal point for management.

The four subtopics capture most of what I think you have to master as a manager in order to run a company, particularly one backed up by solid Back of the Envelope and Vision–Strategy–Execution thinking. They are: management of *people*, *systems*, *processes*, and *funds*. We'll look at managing people in the remainder of this chapter, and we'll examine management of systems and processes and of funds in detail in the following two chapters.

These four points also cover most of what you'll read under the broad heading of management in business. And the Vision-Strategy-Execution Model, again, gives us some help in thinking about how to address these responsibilities.

While the grist for leadership lies in the anchoring vision and in the more general parts of strategy, the underpinnings for effective management are found in the more detailed parts of strategy—the parts that start to outline how, specifically, the general strategic idea will work—and in the follow-through of execution. These are represented in the diagram by the right half of the center circle and all of the following one.

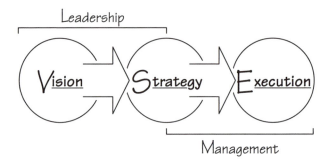

While leadership is about aligning aspirations and beliefs, management is about ensuring actions and activities. These actions and activities determine, in turn, the resources that the business will need and how it will use them in achieving its mission.

Managing People

The American workforce of today is simply amazing. The intersection of our country's commitment to education over the past hundred years with our emergent culture of equal opportunity and human rights has created a population with the highest potential that the world has ever known. Our challenge as managers is no longer simply how to deploy the hands and mold the attitudes that people bring to our businesses—the challenge Henry Ford alluded to with his comment about wanting to hire only the hands of his assembly-line employees and not their minds. Rather, the challenge of today's manager is how to establish the settings and the circumstances that will support employees in figuring out on their own how to contribute their fullest.

I'm convinced that today's employees want to do the right things to contribute to your business's success. And I believe that most individuals who don't appear to fit this characterization are that way because of bad management in the past.

So, how does today's manager capitalize on the amazing potential of the people around her? It begins with how she thinks about herself. For starters, I believe that the whole idea of "the boss" is irrelevant today. Today's workforce has not been educated or conditioned to subject themselves to a "boss." I feel the same way about the whole idea of "reporting to." People today want to work with and support a senior colleague. Few in today's workforce aspire to report to a boss.

If you need to feel like a boss with others reporting to you, you shouldn't be in charge of people in this century. What the managers of people in the twenty-first century need as their driving motivation, rather than authority, is a deep-seated interest in the well-being, in the potential, and in the growth of their businesses and of the people whose lives they touch.

Invariably, people imprint intensely on the person who holds the most senior position in their organization. And they do it involuntarily, regardless of whether the model is a good one or a bad one. Only after seeing many different examples of this phenomenon at work do you notice this influence. It's that imperceptible to the people involved, but it's there.

Consciously or not, people in business organizations are acutely tuned in to the motives and moves of the individual they perceive as the most senior. What they are looking for, I believe, are clues about how to succeed. And they adapt, subconsciously. How much time employees spend at this depends on how clear the signals are from the top. When messages about the company's direction and priorities are obscure, or worse, inconsistent, you can bet that a significant part of most peoples' days are centered on figuring out how to read and how to reflect, or alternatively on how to deflect, the behavior of those in charge, rather than on their jobs.

This is what makes a change at the top such an unsettling event in most businesses. After a while, most people find a comfortable way of adapting themselves to the motives and moves of the person at the top. A change means that their often hard-won *modus operandi* may no longer be effective, and trial and error as a method for adjusting to a new person in charge can be a risky undertaking. Hence the hesitation that most employees experience when there are changes at the top.

But there are also important findings here for executives who have been around a while. People are watching you. They are watching more intensely than you would ever imagine for every clue thay can glean about how to act and what to do. They are studying you so intently that things you might not even know you've done can send shock waves through your workforce, carrying with them either positive or negative effects.

And your personal influence doesn't stop at work. Things you do, the way you act, and who you are affects not only an employee's life at work, but also her life at home. And it's the same for every individual within your sphere of responsibility. Someone once said that when the boss has a bad day, everyone else has three. Think about it. If one in three days is a bad one for you, what's life like for everyone else in the company? And what's it like for their spouses and kids? What's it like for your own spouse and children?

So, what do you do with this insight? The first thing to recognize is that managing people starts with managing yourself. Your own values and your own behaviors are the most powerful tools you have for influencing others.

There are three principles for living your life that I believe are requisite values for anyone running a business today. Together, they constitute solid guides for managing yourself in both your business and in your personal life. My insistence on these values in businesses I've run doesn't come from any moral bias I might have, but rather is a reflection of broad and prevailing trends that have taken place in our society over the past fifty years. These principles for living are a recognition of where our culture is headed today regarding how, generally, people want to think of themselves and want to be treated. Living them assiduously is imperative if you want to unlock the best that your employees have to offer; these three principles are integrity, fairness, and respect.

Integrity

Integrity is simple. It means doing what you say you'll do and having that align with the values you espouse. A lot of people talk about integrity as "doing the right thing." It's hard to disagree with this as an aspirational idea. It's just not an accurate definition of integrity. And it is a principle that I find difficult to put into use, because my definition of "the right thing to do" in a particular circumstance might not be the same as yours. So, what I might see as an act of unimpeachable integrity, you might see as an abrogation of an implicit trust. That's why I like the definition of doing what you say you'll do—some people would say this idea, alone, is reliability—coupled with the unswerving adherence to a clear set of values. That combination makes the most sense to me. And it's something you can control.

People might argue with the rightness or wrongness of what you do, and, hopefully, in your organization there will be a way for them to be heard. But if they see you as always anchoring your commitments in a consistent set of core values and purpose, and then delivering on those commitments, you will reduce their guessing about you to a tolerable level. People will be able to read you clearly and will have the opportunity to decide for themselves whether you are the kind of person for whom they want to work. You'll also set a useful standard for yourself and for those who choose to be a part of your team.

In order to reinforce the principle of integrity, I seek opportunities to clearly anchor the commitments I make to core values, to deliver on those promises, and then to remind people of what I said, why I said it, and what I did so they have a model of follow-through. I also go out of my way to recognize others who do the same, even for small things.

When I walk a plant floor, as I love to do, people will often come up to me and ask a question that I can't answer at the moment. I tell them I'll get back to them by a certain time. I write the commitment down in the pocket notepad I keep just for this purpose. And I get back to them. On time. With an answer anchored in our core values and purpose. My behavior encourages them to do the same, and when they do, I recognize them for their actions. I tell them how important it is for us all to reinforce the priciple of integrity as a pillar of our culture. It can involve the slightest of things, but it makes a huge difference, because the word spreads and soon others start doing the same.

Fairness

The second of the three principles that I believe are requisite values for anyone running a business today is fairness. Once again, fairness is a pretty simple idea. To me, fairness means treating everyone in the same circumstance the same way. It's amazing how we've gotten away from this basic idea, particularly in business structures where we perceive and accept that rank has its privileges.

It's true that some people have offices and others don't. Some work the day shift and others the night. Some get paid more than others. Those differences are not about fairness. They're about the realities of what it takes to execute the business. What's not fair is different pay for people who do the same job, a better office for one manager versus another, and reserved parking spots. Everyone should have access to the same parking spaces. If you are a big shot and arrive late, tough luck! Maybe you'll figure something out on the walk to the door.

There are few things I've ever done in organizations that have had as much impact as intervening in unfair practices. And the changes to unfair practices don't all have to involve big issues: Small things like parking spots, the cleanliness of bathrooms—why should a plant floor bathroom be any less clean than one in the executive suite—and lunchrooms, or the rotation of shifts get the message across. But the big issues, and there surely will be some, are where your commitment to the principle of fairness will be tested most stridently.

For example, when I was CEO of a business where I'd started down the road of promoting fairness, it didn't take long for a group of supervisors to muster their courage, come to my office, and explain what they felt to be a long history of favoritism regarding supervisor pay. My investigation revealed merit in their argument. Among thirty-some supervisors, some were paid up to twice as much as others, and many of the lower-paid supervisors oversaw more workers in more critical areas of production than their higher-paid counterparts. There was no logical structure to the payscale.

The most underpaid supervisors had previously been hourly employees, and in extreme cases their salaries ended up actually lower than they would have been, including overtime, if the employees had declined the "promotions" and remained hourly workers. At the other extreme, among the highest-paid supervisors were our most recent hires. The argument here was a familiar one: "That's what we need to pay to compete for quality talent in the market."

This company was not in a position to add to its costs. Our business plan for survival depended upon just the opposite. So what do you do? The answer really wasn't all that hard. First, I assembled all of our supervisors, presented the facts, and let them know that I did not believe our current practice was fair. Next, I showed them an analysis of our total expenditures on supervisor pay, compared with what our human resources department said it would cost if we hired all new employees. There was a gap. It was significant, but not enormous. Then I explained the reality of the circumstance, the principle of fairness, and the corresponding decision:

> "Ladies and gentlemen, we have a business plan to which we all contributed and that we can not violate. We also have discovered an issue of unfairness in supervisor pay. Our solution must be to treat everyone in the same circumstance the same way, recognizing differences in job contributions with differences in pay as best we can until we get the company back on its feet. Here is a new schedule of pay, without names, that better matches supervisor compensation with job contributions and responsibilities. As you will see, the pay for some positions will go up and for others it will go down, but the result stays within our budget. Here also is our human resource manager's analysis of the gap between our total supervisor pay package and market pay. My commitment is to attempt to bridge the gap with proceeds from improved company performance as soon as possible, and I will report back to you on our progress every quarter. I hope that everyone will value being part of a fair system, and continue on the team. If, however, anyone chooses to move on, we respect your decision and wish you the best. Please let me know of your decision within forty-eight hours."

About two thirds of the supervisors—an even mix of compensation gainers and losers—signed on at the meeting, excited about the swiftness and openness of the decision. Another eight or so followed suit the next day. Four chose to leave. Within sixty hours we had replaced the four we lost by promoting worthy candidates from within, and morale took a measurable jump. Within a year, we were at market pay. Talk about winning the hearts of the rank and file!

Your obvious intention and unswerving follow-through in protecting the principle of fairness can be the most solid and enduring anchor for the mantle of leadership that your organization bestows upon you. The sacred trust of fairness, however, can never be breached without major damage to your stature. Once you have established fairness as a principle, your employees will hold you to an impeccable standard, not maliciously, but because they want so deeply to believe that what you stand for is real. Treating everyone in the same circumstance the same way means exactly that, and, as in my example of the supervisors' pay changes, it can be painful at times. I've also had to make the tough decision to terminate valuable senior colleagues who inadvertently breached standards for which others had lost jobs. But if you believe in the principle, you protect it at all costs.

Respect

The example of supervisor pay wasn't just an example of fairness, it also was an example of respect. Respect means dealing with people in such a way that they feel valued. This doesn't mean everyone has to be consulted on every decision. Nor does it mean that you can't deliver discipline or take positions that other people don't like. If that were the case we wouldn't need CEOs, presidents, division heads, supervisors, and the like, we'd only need pollsters.

Some people misinterpret respect as being nice. When confronted with the need to deliver bad news, they hem and haw, pass out a lot of compliments, and are unclear about the message, hoping that the resulting ambiguity will be easier for the other person to deal with than the reality. This isn't being respectful. It isn't even being nice.

Respect starts with the presumption that the other person is as competent as you are, and that he is smart enough and tough enough to deal with reality. Protecting someone from reality is one of the worst forms of disrespect, because it doesn't give the other person the chance to deal with the situation. You are presuming the person to be weak without having the courage to let him know it. And putting off a difficult discussion almost always results in compounding a bad result. If you respect me, tell me the truth. And tell me now. I'll do the same for you. This posture conveys more than sweet words in expressing how much you believe in and value the person you're talking to.

Another category of respect, which comes into play in work settings and for which you are responsible, is respect for the organization. It's difficult to maintain respect for your organization among your employees unless you set the standard you wish them to follow. This means living according to the same rules they do. It means never deriding your business. It means defending and supporting it at all costs. It means no back-channel gossip about someone else. It means doing what you say you will do.

My favorite part of some days are conversations on the plant floor or in the shop. It's a time to listen to people and to show them that the organization cares about their points of view. By following up with them in writing or by having a follow-up conversation, you demonstrate to your employees how you want them to deal with others—out of respect for the business.

Integrity, Fairness, and Respect Together

There's a difference between appreciating integrity, fairness, and respect in the abstract and living them as ideals. Make a small sign that says "INTEGRITY, FAIRNESS, RESPECT," and tape it to the frame of your computer screen. Focus on it for just a minute at the beginning and at the end of every day for a week. You'll find yourself thinking of things that you can do to improve in your management of others. You will make a difference in your effectiveness as a leader and as a manager. But the very best thing about living the principles of integrity, fairness, and respect in your job is seeing others start to do the same.

I'll never forget, after a few weeks as a new turn-around CEO, overhearing a conversation among a group of five or six factory workers who were meeting informally to solve a problem that bridged their areas of respective responsibility. One asked, "What's the most fair thing to do here?" A moment later another answered, "Whatever we do we've got to do it quickly and in a way that everyone understands our thinking." This comment was followed by, "And we've got to make sure that whatever we do is in sync with what everyone's been told before now."

I still get a little choked up thinking about that moment. Not only was I proud of what was taking place, but I also knew that a new style of working was emerging that would have a profound effect on everyone's life at work, and that the future of the company was looking up.

Postscript on Leadership and Management

Are great leaders and managers born or developed? It's such an over-asked and over-answered question that unless I thought I had a particularly interesting angle, I'd never raise it. So, what's my answer? It is neither and both. Neither innate talent nor hard-earned skill is sufficient. And both are required.

There's a lot to be learned, mostly from the experiences of others, in order to become as good as you can be at managing businesses and people. And I can think of no other profession to which one could dedicate themselves more completely, where there would still be so much left to learn when it's time to call it quits.

On the other hand, I am absolutely convinced that the most critical ingredients to success in these two endeavors—leadership and management—are pretty simple. They are common sense and decent values. Common sense and decent values can be learned, but at some level the combination of one's genes and the accumulation of one's past experiences either add up to excellence in these areas, or they add up to something less.

A lot of people survive in leadership and management roles with something less. More survive without any formal attention to what can be learned. But few of these kinds of CEOs, presidents, and managers ever reach anything close to their full potential, nor do they provide all that they could to those who work for them to help them reach their own potential. But you can. It's as easy as asking yourself, every day, "Am I the kind of person for whom I would like to work? Would working for me inspire me to be better than I might be otherwise? Would I look forward to coming to work for me? Would I be proud to have my family and friends watching a movie of me at work? If I worked for me would I be excited a the end of the day to go home and tell my spouse and kids about my day at work?" Simply bringing these questions into your consciousness makes all the difference. And when you do, being on the right side of the answers to these questions, all the time, is not as hard as you might think.

How might your own life be different, and how might the lives of those who work with you be different, if you had effectively installed credible Back of the Envelope and Vision-Strategy-Execution thinking and an inspired culture of renewal in your business? If you had conditioned your team to seek, rather than avoid, renewal opportunities? And if, upon that platform, you had begun to excel as a trusted leader and manager of your people?

Please take just a minute to pause here. Before you continue reading, close your eyes and shut out all other thoughts. Ask yourself how it would feel to be a trusted leader in a renewal-oriented company. When you open your eyes, tell yourself that everything you've just imagined is possible. It's all a matter of will. Your own.

Chapter 9

Inspired Operations

So, how to spread your positive influence as a leader into the day-to-day operations of your business and into the lives and motivations of everyone who works for you? You do this by aligning your processes and control systems with your Back of the Envelope and Vision–Strategy–Execution frameworks and with your intent to create a culture of renewal.

Aligning Processes and Control Systems

Whether you are running an ice cream stand or a large manufacturing operation, there is already a complex set of processes and control systems in place that determines how things get done. Some of this might have been put in place consciously, but some is likely happenstance. Regardless, most will have been in place for quite some time. Lots of things in most businesses are just done the way they have always been done in the past. Habits are sticky that way. And in most businesses, adjustments to past practices are discouraged, either openly or subtly, rather that encouraged.

Accordingly, opportunities exist in every mainstream business to improve the ways things are done by better aligning processes, policies, and control systems with a fresh look at your Back of the Envelope and Vision–Strategy–Execution frameworks. The payoffs here can be big—big enough that thinking about how things get done needs someone's continuous attention. Solid thinking at the top is not sufficient for admirable results; rather, the degree of synchronization between solid thinking at the top and optimal processes, policies, and control systems makes the difference between the highest-performing, highest-profit companies and those that are left behind.

Unfortunately, relatively few managers in mainstream businesses spend much time thinking about their processes, policies, and control systems. It's too easy to be okay with the way things have been done in the past. And the details of how things actually get done sounds below the realm of many CEOs' responsibilities.

Yet, when you think about it, the job at the top is all about being responsible for what gets done and how. Your work with the Back of the Envelope and with vision and strategy, along with your commitment to renewal, are critical preambles. But where the rubber meets the road is in the substance of execution. Again, it is the effectiveness of your processes, policies, and control systems that determines whether your business actually capitalizes on your higher-level thinking, or whether those principles will stand as interesting but peripheral abstractions, separate from what actually gets done, with little effect on the results you deliver.

Another argument I often hear is that process improvement through policies and control systems is the stuff of specialist consultants. That kind of thinking, coupled with a reluctance to spend on outsiders, is responsible for underperformance in many mainstream businesses.

While inefficiencies in the way things are done are well understood at the points of their occurrence, they have a way of remaining under the radar of those in charge. They're not addressed because the people at the top don't understand the basics of process, policies, and control system optimization. That's why you need to be something of an expert, or need to have someone on staff or on retainer with expertise in this territory.

Let's start with some definitions:

- Processes are the agreed-upon ways of doing things.
- Policies document and memorialize the processes.

In some businesses the key processes and their corresponding policies are assembled in a formal manual. But in many mainstream businesses they exist only as an unconsolidated legacy of departmental memos and tribal knowledge. Some processes and the policies that memorialize them may be monitored, with adherence tracked explicitly and on a regular basis. But others have been around so long, or seem so obvious, that they are never monitored. They are never challenged. Even after the people closest to the action know that the processes and policies have become outdated, they live on as guidelines that may or may not be operative. All this goes on "below the radar screen" of managers further up the line, who may have great misconceptions about what is actually happening in their businesses.

When they are current and well organized, good policies and processes make it easier to transform newcomers into productive employees. They also make it easier for veterans to live by the rules and to recognize when it's time to make some changes. Taking orders, assigning tasks, receiving parts, creating distribution timetables, deciding warranty terms, setting pricing, managing vendors, reviewing employee performance, awarding performance bonuses, and so on are all processes that are backed up to varying degrees, depending upon the company, by formal policies. If someone breaks a good policy and fails to follow the corresponding process, generally nothing shuts down. Life goes on. But often the work continues with lower and lower levels of efficiency and productivity, which usually translate to lower financial performance. This growing inefficiency is often neither seen nor understood by management.

Are you okay living with this reality in your business? If not, then who in your business is responsible for processes and policies? Who will attend to their enforcement and to changing outdated processes to maintain optimal efficiency in your day-to-day business? In the absence of another designee, that job is yours.

Control systems are different from processes and policies. Compliance with processes and policies is a matter of individual choice; individuals choose to either follow or to break the "rules." Control systems take away that latitude. They are governors that set limits around critical processes to ensure the processes don't exceed certain "safe" boundaries of operation. Some are "hard wired," as in previous generations of machine controls that prevent operations outside specified ranges. Others, increasingly, are computer-based.

When critical processes exceed the ranges set by control systems, the reactions are usually sharper and swifter than the general, and sometimes not-so-apparent, declines in productivity that result from inefficiencies in process and a lack of enforced policy. Breeches of control systems usually trigger shutdowns, alarm bells, or some other unmistakable alert to whomever might be responsible for what's going on.

Most computer software is heavy with control systems. If you exceed the tolerance for inputs, for example, things shut down. Modern control systems for plant machinery work the same way. Adjust a setting beyond the prescribed range, and the machine shuts down.

The responsibility for processes, policies, and control systems can be a big job, even in a small business. Part of the art of running any organization lies in deciding which functions need which levels of backup. Because of the usual lack of attention of mainstream CEOs to this area, I now expect to find big mismatches in most of the businesses I inspect—outdated control systems on things that don't matter any more, with only cursory policies that document roughly proscribed processes for those things that make the most difference. All of these processes need to be rethought as the business operations change with the evolution of the Back of the Envelope and Vision–Strategy–Execution frameworks.

Most simply, then, processes, policies, and control systems are all part of effective execution, the third part of the Vision–Strategy–Execution model. They are the assurances that what gets executed lines up with the first two elements of the framework.

Taking into consideration, however, the full range of tasks necessary to operate the business, and the likelihood of existing mismatches between oversight and needs, where do you start? How do you think about synchronizing all of these tasks so that the resulting processes reinforce one another and align with what actually gets done?

The approach here is Miesian. Mies van der Rohe was a famous architect of the International Style, whose design theme and signature phrase was, "Less is more." It's like that with processes, policies, and control systems. Less is more. Begin by picking the handful of core processes upon which the success of your strategies rests, and address these first. Define the optimum processes and record them. The descriptions need not be long. The shorter, the better. Just make sure they are brutally clear. Then choose the signals that will tell you if the processes stray out of your specified operating range. Decide whether you are comfortable relying on a policy to assure compliance, or whether you need a control system. Many of the CEOs I've worked with assemble the signals that indicate adherence to their key policies and control systems into a daily "flash report" that summarizes the performance of each key process, according to its prescribed operating range, on one page, every day, for the previous day's operations. It's a good idea.

And how hard is all of this if you will be the standard setter and gate-keeper, as many CEOs, presidents, and general managers are in mainstram companies? The answer is that it depends. Not on how smart you are, nor on how committed you are to getting your execution right. The answer depends upon whether you have built a strong sense of vision and a com-pelling strategy that pervades your business. If you have, there will be a simpler set of items that need formal monitoring. Your people will already have a clear sense of what they need to accomplish and will be inspired to get it done. They'll understand how their individual actions contribute to the desired outcome. And they'll have a solid understanding of the bound-aries of acceptable and unacceptable behaviors and ways of doing things to deliver the goal.

If you have done a good job with vision and strategy, people closest to the action will be the best judges of the effectiveness of their own processes and will establish policies and control systems on their own. In these set-tings, it becomes the frontline employees, not you, who will be continuously challenging, experimenting, and finding better ways of doing things, and institutionalizing the best of their findings in their own workplaces. This leaves for you the overarching responsibilities, those that cross departmen-tal lines or extend beyond the boundaries of the workers' control.

This ideal of distributed responsibility for processes, policies, and con-trol systems is a high goal in execution. But there is a solid body of thought regarding how to put this practice in place in your business, and you'll find it embedded in the cortex of virtually all of the best-run businesses in America. Upon examination, such shared responsibility is not such a high bar to clear in companies where it derives from solid thinking about the Back of the Envelope plan and about vision and strategy. So, why not make it a part of your business?

A New Approach to Managing Processes—What's Kaizen?

As part of the Allied post-war reconstruction effort in Japan, a young American named Edward Deming found fertile ground for planting his theoretical seeds for a new approach to business execution. Over a period of roughly four decades, Japanese businesses nurtured Demming's ideas, creating an omnibus philosophy of management that has become known as lean manufacturing. While the thrust of the lean approach was initially focused on manufacturing operations, and particularly on plant floor processes and systems, the ideas are just as applicable to nonmanufacturing activities, including things like sales, customer service, finance and accounting, engineering, distribution, and the like. In fact, the most powerful ideas from the lean manufacturing philosophy work almost anywhere.

The place to start exploring lean in your business as a path to more effective processes, policies, and control systems is with a practice called Kaizen. Kaizen is the idea of continuous improvement. But the challenge with embracing this idea in many companies is that it flies directly in the face of the foundational concepts of organizational structure and management science that dominated business thinking from the time of Henry Ford's production line through the 1960s and most of the 1970s. Much of established business leaders' conflict with Kaizen arises from the fact that the initiative resides at the point where the work is done, and not in the head office.

Kaizen execution attacks the beliefs that (1) there is a "best way" to do most anything, (2) that the best way to do something can be discovered by the smartest people in management, and (3) that once it's found you can institutionalize it with a high level of comfort in its effectiveness over a long period of time. The premise of Kaizen is that the best people to develop or improve processes, policies, and control systems, and to continuously tweak them for optimum performance, are the ones closest to the work. Kaizen posits that folks further up the line ought to give frontline workers the freedom, the encouragement, and the tools, within certin boundaries, to experiment with getting better.

Kaizen execution simply says that workers are smarter than corporate planners and analysts, at least when it comes to optimizing how they do their work. Because they occupy the best positions to diagnose inefficiencies and to conceptualize effective remedies, they already know more about process improvement—though they might not call it that—than you'd ever imagine. And they've already figured out solutions to a lot of the things you worry about. The problem is that few managers in mainstream businesses ever ask them for their thoughts or give them the go-ahead and the tools to try their own solutions. Most managers don't see it as part of their jobs to listen to how the people doing the work think it ought to be done.

The sad result is that frontline employees continue to toil under outdated control systems and policies that force them to follow no-longer-relevant processes. What a shame!

Kaizen execution rejects this outcome. In fact, it turns it inside out. Kaizen is anchored in two principles that must be soulfully embraced at the very top of your organization in order for the exercise not to be a waste of everyone's time. If you can't get solidly behind these two principles and behind the fundamental ideas of entrusting responsibility to those most capable of dealing with it and of igniting their inspiration in your business, read no further.

The first principle that you need to embrace, and I mean really embrace, is that people are smart. Sure, they'll make mistakes, and some will be significant. But it's intent that counts, particularly over time. A corollary principle you must embrace is that your staff's intention is to do a good job.

The Kaizen approach to unlocking peoples' ingenuity and their intentions to do a good job revolves around installing a culture of trial and error. Every job in your organization needs to add an extra dimension, like a radar signal that oscillates broadly at first, then narrows so that it can zero in on an exact fix. People need to feel inspired not only to continue to deliver their results according to current expectations through the processes, policies, and control systems already in place, but they also need to be encouraged to experiment with their ideas. If some of the things smart people try don't fail, they're not thinking broadly enough. But with the right support and encouragement, they'll eventually get it right. Then they'll keep it right through what Kaizen and lean manufacturing call continuous improvement and what I have come to think of as the narcotic of self actualization at work. This optimal work atmosphere can drive the levels of effectiveness, productivity, and operating results in your business to levels that you will never achieve in any lesser way.

The second principle of Kaizen, one that also needs to be evident in the DNA at the top of your organization, is that people care about what they do at work and they want to work as productively as possible. People want to be proud of how they spend their time at work, and they want to make a difference for their peers, their companies, their families, and their communities.

We have all carried around, for much of our careers, the notion that the only way to get people to do their best is to make it worth their while. You have to pay them something extraordinary to get them to do better than average. That's just not true. There are too many examples of the contrary. The major incentives in Kaizen execution are simple. Let people know how they're doing, frequently and in real time if possible. Allow employees to set their own goals for improvement. Free them to use their own wits, within reasonable limits and without risking current productivity, to achieve their goals. And give them the tools and encouragement to do so. The payoffs will be self-evident, and will be visible not only in your production figures, but also in your employees' satisfaction with their own successes and in their enthusiasm for their jobs.

The most powerful motivators you can give your people are your trust in their ability to figure some things out on their own, and your recognition of their achievements when they do so. Doing more than recognizing their results, and particularly tying pay to results, has a curious way of becoming a disincentive, rather than a motivator, over time. And eventually it backfires.

Most people take their greatest pride from simply doing a terrific job, no matter what it is, and being recognized for it. That's how it works on a Saturday morning when your spouse asks you to fix the screen door and then showers you with praise for doing a great job. It's the same at work. There are just too many examples of people at all levels turning down significant increases in pay in order to remain with a company where their potential to contribute is recognized and supported. There are too many for me to believe that the best way to ensure performance is through financial bribery. If that's all you've got, your vision and your strategy still need work. Of course, financial rewards are always appreciated. But in the best-run companies money is secondary to what motivates employees' burning desires to do a great job. And creating that environment is your job.

Another New Angle on Managing—What a Waste!

"No-waste" execution is another core concept of lean that is closely related to Kaizen. In the language of lean, waste is defined as anything that does not contribute directly to customer value. Scrap is an obvious example. It benefits no one and the costs, when fully appreciated in many operations, can be staggering. Less obvious than scrap, but nonetheless often more costly, is nonproductive time, both of people and of equipment. Think for a moment about two things: the productive use of your own time in the last twenty-four hours and the productive use of a typical factory or office worker's time. How many of your moments over the last twenty-four hours actually contributed to something that would be seen by a customer as adding value?

In organizations that have not embraced the no-waste execution mantra, the standard is estimated to be in the 30 to 40 percent range. That's the value-adding time, not the waste time! Why? It's simply because we don't think about it very much. We've grown so accustomed to such a pitiful level of contribution that we don't even think about how to do better. As important as no-waste execution is to efficiency and profitability, it's just not a bright enough signal on our radar screens. Other things, things that either don't contribute directly to customer perceived value or that contribute less than the reduction of waste, occupy a majority of our attention through the day. No-waste execution in operating processes, policies, and control systems represents a hidden treasure for most mainstream businesses. And no-waste execution thinking is at the same time the map and the expedition for finding this treasure.

Over the past decade a number of excellent prescriptive texts have been written about how to put these two powerful ideas together—Kaizen and the elimination of waste. Typically, they lay out lengthy sequences of steps to replicate the processes as they are performed in model Japanese and American businesses, including advice on team selection and team building, group meeting guidelines, measuring techniques, and the like.

But like most other things in mainstream businesses, the essence— enough to get you started—is pretty much common sense. To capitalize on the full potential of no-waste execution, you'll need to commit to developing a deeper understanding of lean theory and what's worked and hasn't worked for others. But mainstream businesses can gain a lot just by introducing the Kaizen and no-waste principles in their simplest forms. Beyond that, the benefits you derive will depend upon your own level of interest and your commitment to learning more about these ideas as tools for improving your business's execution of its strategy and increasing the likelihood it will achieve its mission.

A Team of Champions

If you choose to start down the road to lean, your first step toward the benefits of Kaizen and no-waste execution will be diagnostic. Identify the most likely targets for improving execution. Discuss these with your key reports, and then engage a team of champions to explore the application of Kaizen and no-waste principles in one area of your business.

The key considerations for picking your team of champions has less to do with organizational position than with the credibility of the members in the eyes of others, and with selfless, intellectual curiosity. You know the opinion leaders in your workforce. You also know who is more concerned with helping others and helping the business improve performance than with recognition for his personal achievements. You also know who has inherent leadership qualities. Pick these people as your champions.

Ideally, the resulting pool will include no one in a senior position. It's better for this to be a bottom-up initiative. Your part, and the part of other members of your senior team, is to support your champions in their new role with your knowledge, with your interest, and with your sponsorship.

Generally, your team of champions in a business of a hundred to a few hundred employees involves around half a dozen members. In the smallest of businesses you still need two or three. At the outset, participation can be a collateral duty, though later on the results can warrant full-time assignments for some. Ideally, every champion will already be somewhat familiar with the lean philosophy. But to put everyone on a level playing field, give each member one of the excellent overview texts on lean, and make sure that you and the other members of your senior team read it too.

Next, assemble your champions for the first time to share thoughts about what they've read and to begin talking about where and how to pilot lean in your organization. This initial discussion about the prospect of introducing lean usually goes in two directions.

One is general, and is about the challenges the company can expect in fitting the overall process into your particular circumstances. What else is going to have to change in order for these initiatives to have a chance? Who's going to welcome the changes? Who's going to resist? This is a useful discussion, because everyone believes that her organization is unique. But it's also a discussion that seldom leads to a prescription that varies much from the textbook guidelines. While it's important to give your champions some time to express both general optimism and concerns, this isn't the part of discussion that adds the most value.

The second direction is the more valuable. It's about where, specifically, to start, and it may or may not end up zeroing in on the targets you initially chose. That's okay. Unless there is some compelling reason to do otherwise, go with the group's recommendation.

Two additional tips come into play here that I believe are critical. The first is to begin this exercise without fanfare. Don't make big announcements or promises of great things to come. It's far better for this movement to gain momentum through its early stages as a subtle, no-big-deal kind of thing. The effort should appear tangential and will hopefully go unnoticed by people other than those involved.

My second bit of strong advice is to start where you believe you will have the highest likelihood of success, regardless of how modest it might be. Matching up with the "low visibility" guideline, this usually means beginning with a small, not-so-complex, and not-so-highly visible part of your operations.

In a recent example, I picked a self-contained manufacturing feeder function located in a room that was separate from the rest of the plant. The people who worked in that room often felt left out and underappreciated because of their isolation, and they were highly honored and enthusiastic about participating in the team. The combination of their location and their relative self-sufficiency constituted a lab that operated as a "safe haven" for refining our techniques through learning-by-doing. When questions came from other employees about what was going on in the special shapes area, I simply told the truth: We would be running a trial that we thought might have merit for wider application, if we could get it to work there. For those few more curious souls, we held nothing back in explaining as much of the idea as they wanted to hear. But after the first few days, the work went mostly unnoticed by others, though the participants remained riveted by their tasks and ecstatic about their opportunity.

Once you've done your diagnostic work—assembled your team of champions and picked your initial point of focus—the first active step is to analyze how work is currently being done. Leave it to your team of champions to collaborate with the relevant workforce in mapping the flows and usages of labor and materials, and in measuring initial levels of productivity in units of output per unit of time. In fact, they should be measuring almost everything in the target function. A stopwatch, click-counters, a whiteboard, and lots of charting paper are requisite tools. Check in with your team daily at first, then every two to three days, to learn what they're discovering. This will be an exciting and revealing experience in most instances, because it confirms to the workers what many have suspected all along. And it's their opportunity to telegraph it directly to you. Waste abounds!

Keeping track of how much employee time is spent actually adding value to products or services, versus how much is spent waiting for someone else to finish a task, waiting for or looking for parts or information, waiting for a machine to become available or be fixed, cleaning up, filling out forms, or redoing something will surprise you. I heard a statistic recently that over the course of the average two- to three-hour football telecast, the ball is in play for less than ten total minutes! The rest of the time is mostly spent standing around! The same idea applies in many business processes. Diversions, waiting time, excess material and energy, and superfluous tracking and reporting systems add precious little to customer satisfaction.

Through their inaugural experiment with Kaizen and no-waste principles, your team should be on the lookout for two kinds of metrics. The first involves those measurements that document and track the productivity of the key subprocesses of the target operation. The second are metrics that indicate overall productivity. As an example, in a simple manufacturing target area, where you are looking to gauge the effectiveness of the subroutines, you might consider measuring things like absenteeism, on-time reporting for work, good versus bad raw materials, wait time for parts, machine setup or adjustment time, tool and machine production time per hour, rework as a percentage of total production, quality rejects, lost time accidents, "hands on machines time," staging, and outgoing transfer times. The metrics for overall productivity of the target operation might include things like units of output per labor hour, average process time per unit of output, and total quality production per hour, per employee, and per shift.

An example from MW Windows illustrates this idea. After a period of work process analysis, conducted by mapping and measuring activity, the team of champions eventually zeroed in on the metric of "Sales Dollars Per Labor Hour" as the overarching indicator of total plant productivity and of the effectiveness of operations. It was the simple calculation of the total sales dollar value created by a single shift divided by the labor hours incurred on the shift. Eventually, it would be calculated for each of thirty-four separate manufacturing centers in the plant, for all three shifts. Each supervisor picked three to six key indicators to record hourly and per shift. Supervisors tallied and added each shift's daily result to a prominent, chart-sized trend line and bar graph in the ten to fifteen minutes following each shift, and then shared their on-the-spot diagnoses and results with their incoming replacements. They repeated the recap with their own team at the start of the next day's shift and entertained a brief period for comments and discussion by their crews. They also stopped wasting time on bins full of other reports that had been put in place over the years to give management some idea of what was going on. Nobody read these any more anyway.

As ideas for improvement surfaced from the groups at MW, most were performed as trials in controlled circumstances and then were immediately evaluated against the Sales Dollars Per Labor Hour record of the previous few days and of the same day the previous year. The ideas for improvement at MW included things like assembling parts in shift batches and locating them next to work stations, moving equipment around to minimize reach and transfer distances, reconfiguring bins for fasteners to accommodate vendor-managed inventory, redefining job descriptions, cross-training, and job rotation. Only the fixes that required a corresponding adjustment by another department or that required resources beyond those already provided in the shift budget—every shift had a discretionary budget for process improvements—required approval.

Successful ideas from all of the manufacturing subunits were discussed daily at a mid-morning meeting of the lead supervisors, where overall company performance on Sales Dollars per Labor Hour was reviewed and ideas for plant-wide implementations were evaluated and agreed upon.

The response was amazing. Within six weeks, it became routine to find one or two shift crews either staying late or coming in early, on their own time, to work out an idea. Prominent charts showed everyone's progress. And team pride, along with a friendly, softball-league-type rivalry among teams, emerged.

Within ninety days, Sales Dollars per Labor Hour had jumped in many operations from lower $40s to mid $40s. A year later, supervisors were embarrassed at the daily meeting if their metric hadn't improved by 50 percent. Two years later, I touched base with the director of operations, one of the most talented and likeable men with whom I have ever had the privilege to serve, for an update. In his last week, a little more than three years after we started, he me told the plant averaged $84 in Sales Dollars per Labor Hour. Think about it: Over a three-year period, a transformation based on bottom-up knowledge of processes resulted in a doubling of productivity. That's twice the output from the same labor force. And morale soared through the roof. The plant had become the company's most powerful selling tool. The feeling there was electric. Visiting customers would see the energy, and would want to give those people their business. The company had emerged from an unknown into an icon of its industry. Your company can, too.

The Four Fundamental Drivers of Performance

The approaches to measurement, diagnosis, and self-improvement that are usually developed first on plant floors also extend to what I call the four fundamental drivers of performance in all execution operations. These are: safety, quality, delivery, and cost. And the order is important. Very important.

People often say, "What gets measured gets done." This is generally true. But it turns out that what you choose to measure also indicates, in a way that can't be misinterpreted to your employees, what you care about. Leaders who talk a lot about their concern for their people and their company yet only measure profits are not credible. They will never engender followership like that found at MW Windows. Most employees know that what you measure is what you care about. And what you care about is who you are, as far as your employees are concerned.

Safety

For years I ran companies while thinking of safety as a personnel function, sort of in the same category as employee benefits. Not that either of these two are unimportant, but neither of these functions was where I had been inclined to look for improved organizational performance. Safety had seemed to me to be more a result of practices, not a driver of performance. Like a lot of other managers, I would feel dreadful in the wake of a work accident and would go overboard visiting families, sending flowers, and the like. Overall, I saw accidents as something I wanted to avoid, but I didn't think that I could do much to influence safety, and that even if I did, I'd never see the evidence in the bottom line. Boy, was I wrong!

I attribute the opening of my eyes to an extraordinary woman whom I was most fortunate to hire into a position that she made me rename Director of Human Development and Organizational Effectiveness as part of her deal. That's a lot of words for what I had been thinking about as personnel and training. Midmorning on her first day at work, I dropped by her office to see how she was settling in, expecting to find her immersed in personnel policy manuals and insurance plans. To my complete surprise, she hadn't even been there. Instead, she'd reported to the plant floor early enough to catch the changeover from the third to the first shift and had been there ever since. And was she mad! "You didn't tell me that this is a place that doesn't care about its people! You've either got to give me a lot of resources, or I'm not staying," she told me. I couldn't believe my ears. Of course I cared about our people. I took pride in knowing about twelve hundred of them, according to the running list I kept in my notebook, by their first and last names. I personally wrote seventeen hundred birthday cards a year. I was at least five times more approachable and, I think, a lot more likable than the fellow I'd replaced.

But what she was talking about was different. The things I'd been doing were nice, but to her, they didn't really matter. As I learned more from her, I saw that my actions hadn't made as much of an impression as I'd thought. I greatly admired her conviction and didn't want to lose her, so I gave her the first program dollars she asked for. With those dollars she did something that never would have crossed my mind: She began to build what I came to believe was, arguably, one of the most significant pillars in the foundation of an organizational rebirth that resulted in a return on investment too embarrassing to reveal.

That foundational pillar was all about letting people know that we cared about them. And the vehicle for her message, and the target of her initial spending, was safety. Compared with others in our industry, our record of safety was not a discredit. But as she quickly brought me to believe, and later to understand deeply, there is no moral margin of error in safety above zero accidents.

After a few weeks of observing what our new Director of Human Development and Organizational Effectiveness had been doing and how people were responding to her, I found myself solidly on the route to conversion. Then an event, the timing of which still gives me chills, rock-eted me into the wall at the end of the road, and in so doing changed my life. Harshly.

On a sunny midmorning in May, a Tuesday, I was introduced to a mother of two preschoolers. She glowed with as bright and as engaging a smile as I could remember, with sparkling, friendly eyes and a presence that exuded her love and her appreciation for everything in her life. As I extended my right hand in anticipation of embracing hers, she extended her left. After a moment that I could not imagine being superceded in its awkwardness and sadness, I learned that this beautiful young woman had lost her right hand in our plant the year before I had arrived. I wept on the spot. Uncontrollably. I still do when I think of it, as I am right now as I write about it.

There is nothing you can accomplish that takes priority over the respon-sibility you bear, personally, for the well-being of the people who choose to work for you. Nothing else even comes close—not satisfying your bank, your customers, or your investors, not even the very existence of their jobs.

We began our earnest commitment to the well-being of our colleagues in that business with a program called Safe Start. There are many others and they are easy to find. Generally, they all involve employees and super-visors in a daily discussion about safety at work, they identify potential risk situations before they ripen, and they spare no expense in reasonable solutions. If you find a task that cannot be done safely, you simply don't do it anymore until you discover another way.

After a year, our accident rate declined by more than 60 percent. For the next year we set a plant-wide two-year goal of zero lost-time accidents. By the end of that year, as we were making admirable progress toward our goal, our savings in workman's compensation insurance was approaching our program costs, which included some pretty amazing improvements, like higher ambient light levels for reduced eye strain, adjusted work sur-face heights for reduced bending and back strain, repackaging of parts for reduced lifting weight, job rotations to reduce repetitive act deterioration, reconfigurations of storage bins for work-in-process inventory to reduce bending and lifting, automatically retracting blades on all utility knives, cut-to-length parts to reduce sawing, speed governors on forklifts, plant aisles that were widened by 50 percent, redesigned carts for glass handling, free safety glasses and gloves, and a company contribution toward employee purchases of non-skid and steel-toe safety shoes.

All of this attention had an additional benefit: We became seventeen hundred people who cared about each other, truly and deeply.

Quality

By the late 1970s, the total quality revolution was galloping across the United States, advancing the work of Edward Deming. The idea of unrelenting dedication to quality is inextricably entwined with Deming's theories about lean manufacturing, which encompass Kaizen and the elimination of waste. Seen in its best light, quality failure is an example of waste—wasted materials, wasted labor, and wasted plant overhead. And that's when the failure is caught before it goes out the door. Once a quality failure is passed on to your customer, it has consequences that are much more far reaching, including damage to your company's reputation and brand, not to mention your costs of recovery and your customers' costs of disappointing their customers as the result of your failure.

By the time that the quality movement took hold in the United States, our tolerance for quality failure was at an all-time high. One need only think back to the time of disappointing product performance like the inferior safety ratings, repair records, and average vehicle lives of the Chrysler K-Car series, the warranty claims on marine outboard engine fuel injection systems, the poor insulating performance of new houses, the substandard sound quality of overseas phone calls, the low on-time performance of trains, and the lack of freshness of fish and produce at local markets in order to recollect the horrifying standard to which our expectations for quality had declined. We demanded no more, so we received no more.

Deming fought an uphill battle on quality that was heavily weighted against him by incumbent American business and government bureaucracies' investments in past decisions. He had, therefore, experimented with his ideas in the reemerging industrial infrastructure of post-World War II Japan. Only after the United States became exposed to the possibilities of the quality movement, which were being demonstrated overseas and exported here, did it become blindingly apparent that we, as a culture, had been settling for far less than we should have. Hence the rush to quality in the United States, roughly twenty years after its acceptance as a routine way of life in Japan.

In mainstream businesses, however, many have yet to embrace the notion of quality. Many of the excuses for not adopting the principles of the total quality movement in our kinds of businesses are misconceptions:

> I have a hard time getting people to change their ways.

> > It's not your job. It's theirs. It has been my experience that when employees see the improvement of quality as a logical extension of a vision, strategy, and execution that they buy into, they can't wait to begin their own experimentations. All they need is your encouragement and some simple tools, things like quality standards, ways to measure their performance against those standards, and some way of feeling appreciated for the progress they will make—through a process like Kaizen execution. Provide them with these tools and you will be amazed at your employees' enthusiasm for exploring new ways of doing things.

> I can't afford a quality program.

> > It took me a while to become a believer, but now I know for sure that the true cost of quality is either zero or less than zero. Said differently, significant improvements in quality are free. Major improvements more than pay for themselves.
> >
> > This logic runs back to two ideas: no-waste execution and the delight of customers. Most organizations I've worked with are no less than dumbfounded with the results they discover when I ask them to estimate the full cost of "non-quality"—quality failures— in their operations. Some approach paralysis when they extend the exercise to include the costs to their customers. But because people don't think they can do anything about it, they simply accept it. And too many customers simply, quietly shift their business without us ever knowing it.
> >
> > Seldom have I seen a well-crafted quality program not begin paying for itself within eighteen months. Many recoup costs much faster. And it is not unusual to find three to ten times returns in third-year programs.

I don't have anyone who can lead a quality program.

> Read a book. Or take your key operations people to any of the
> hundred two- or three-day quality seminars you can find with-
> out looking too hard. Or hire a consultant to get you started and
> to teach you and your organization how to introduce a program
> yourselves. As with most ideas outlined in business books, a qual-
> ity program needn't be all-encompassing for it to work: Main-
> stream businesses can get most of the benefits from a program
> like quality by adopting just the basics of the principles in their
> operations.
>
> If outside assistance is the route you choose, pick a consultant
> less on the basis of what he knows, and more on the basis of chem-
> istry. By now, nearly anyone who has worked successfully in the
> field knows enough about the philosophy and how to implement
> it to teach it to you and your group. Choose, rather, on the basis of
> how well you think his style and personality will play with your
> team. You should be able to get all the help you need to get started
> down the road to total quality, and learn how to proceed yourself,
> for a fee in the neighborhood of $25,000—that's less than the fully
> loaded cost of a clerical person for a year. Which would you rather
> have?
>
> Feeling like you don't know how to do it is just not a signifi-
> cant barrier.

Programs like that don't stick around here.

> Business improvement programs don't stick only because people
> believe they can make them go away, either by the "limp-leg play
> along" or by actively undermining them. Both of these techniques
> usually work when the program is anchorless and is not seen as a
> logical extension of a greater story of vision, strategy, and execu-
> tion that everyone has bought into.
>
> Your having started with safety also helps you here. By first
> demonstrating your fanatical commitment to their well-being,
> you will encourage your employees to get more deeply committed
> to doing their part to reach their shared aspirations for the busi-
> ness. Their enthusiasm for programs they believe in won't wane.
> But still, there might be outliers. At this point, it will be clear to all

that the outliers need to be working somewhere else. And no one will be more inspired by your taking the appropriate actions than the true believers.

My customers are happy with the quality I give them now.

> Sony, as the story goes, didn't develop the Walkman by asking customers if they were unhappy with their transistor radios. The company created something that was far beyond its customers' abilities to imagine. Most great products and services happen like that.
>
> Never, therefore, will your company rise to greatness by waiting for your customers to tell you their dissatisfactions. They only know, in most instances, what they've experienced. While the mantra of marketing from the 1960s through the 1980s was "listen to your customers," great companies don't just listen to their customers, they lead them.
>
> It's the same with quality. Your customers are very likely to be happy with whatever level of quality you and others currently are providing them, until someone ups the ante. Make it you.

Delivery

From your customers' perspective, the only thing worse than not getting what they need from you is getting it too late to use it in the way they intended. In the collision repair business, late delivery of a vehicle is more disappointing to customers than any other aspect of the service. This is also true of waiting. Somehow we've grown to think that it's okay to make our customers wait until we are ready to serve them. There's a wonderful story, again from automotive aftermarket, about a tire retailer in the Pacific Northwest whose counter help run out into the parking lot to greet customers. The company has the highest customer satisfaction in the industry, an exceptional top-line growth rate, unchallenged customer loyalty, and the highest prices in the market.

In a business-to-business situation, when you're late, it's likely that your customer will disappoint her own customer, and then, adding insult to injury, will have to go through the headache of returning your late shipment and resolving the credit issue. A more subtle, but a much more serious, consequence, I believe, is the blow to your reputation for integrity, reliability, and the level of interest you have demonstrated in your customer's business.

Like a lot of things, the impact of being late might not be felt immediately. If you don't get an irate phone call, you might be tempted to wave it off. But like a series of head traumas, the consequences of being late add up, and are far more significant in today's culture of just-in-time, outsourcing, and zero defects as a way of life in competitive survival.

I earnestly believe that people like to award their business over time to those whom they believe, through demonstrations of behavior, have their best interest at heart. People like to do business with people who will do whatever it takes not to let them down. If this idea feels good to you as you read it, then being late is just not acceptable.

But there is an interesting circular point to be made: Most late deliveries trace back to morale, waste, or quality problems. Solve the morale, waste, and quality problems in your operations, and you'll resolve 90 percent of the causes of missed commitments.

But there will always be that odd "perfect storm" of occurrences, such as the unexpected breakdown that threatens to blow a commitment to a customer despite your best efforts. Rather than thinking of these kinds of jams as horrible events, I've come to think of them as opportunities of a sort. As long as they don't happen very often.

The logic goes like this: Everyone understands that something goes badly for everyone every once in a while. Rather than make excuses or accept these inevitabilities that hit even the best of organizations from time to time as finalities, I look at them as exhilarating challenges. I consider them opportunities not only to recover face, but also to recover in such a way that the subject of our miscue thinks even more of us in the aftermath than she did before. Business teams anchored in solid Back of the Envelope and Vision–Strategy–Execution thinking, who feel safe at work, anticipate renewal, are proud of their quality, and are committed 100 percent not to let their customers down can usually find a way to turn these tables.

This is not to imply that it's easy to recover from a missed commitment. To the contrary, it usually requires an effort above and beyond the call of duty—sometimes extra hours on many peoples' parts, with an intensity of purpose that is unsustainable for long. Heroism you might call it. Winning against the odds. But you do this as a team that is motivated to accomplish something extraordinary for someone else. Because you care. Because you don't want to let them down. And because the entire team believes in the vision, strategy, and execution of your business.

There are two points here. One is that, in matters of timeliness, you can greatly reduce the odds for failure through clear thinking about safety, morale, no-waste principles, and quality. The second is that, in those rare instances when all the odds do stack up against you and when there is only one daunting way out, the right attitudes and culture can forge a group heroism that you can count on to deliver the goods nearly every time. And what a feeling that is!

It's like a narcotic. It's the confidence that comes from living occasionally on the edge of survival. It's the feeling my father used to talk about on those rare occasions when I could get him to recount his years as a combat fighter pilot. There is something spiritually satisfying about knowing you can do things that others are afraid to try—dangerous and important things. And once you've lived through it, the prospect of being tested again, as illogical as it seems to those who haven't been there, becomes deliciously enticing.

Plus, other people find out. When your customer learns what you've done on his behalf, he will be welded to your side. Do it more than once, and he'll be looking for opportunities to reciprocate—to forgive generously in the rare instance when you can't pull off the miracle. But the big multiplier comes on the inside. This is the stuff of legend. It is the substance of company lore. It becomes what people who don't know you hear about you. It's what your employees want to have the chance to demonstrate themselves, and to be a part of, forever.

Cost

Businesses spend huge amounts every year on outsiders, fruitlessly, in their quests for reduced costs. If you can get yourself to the point we've reached so far in running your business, with solid Back of the Envelope, vision and strategy thinking, and the elements of execution that we've covered in place, cost reduction will begin to happen by itself. For free. It's never failed, in my experience.

When people begin feeling, really feeling:

That they are bound together at a deep and fundamental emotional level,

To do something that resonates with how they want to live their lives,

Where they can see a logical path toward its achievement,

In a place that cares for them and where they feel safe,

Where they are proud of the quality of what they're doing,

Where they come to work to serve, and not to let down, someone else,

And where they can be heroes from time to time, they will find the keys to minimizing costs on their own.

They will deliver things that no outside cost-reduction consultant will ever have a chance of finding. Just let them know that the continuous reduction of costs is a requisite for keeping everything else going the way that it is, and they will do it.

In one company I ran for two years, I'd been building for just about seven months on everything that you've read up to here, when I called for cost reduction. Most of the workforce hadn't finished high school, and I sat up the night before the meeting wondering how it was going to go. Would they get it? By asking something of them that they might not be able to handle, would I destroy the underpinnings of the vision and strategy that we had all labored to put in place and held so dear? Was it too big a step? Was it worth the risk? We'd been through a lot. I'd come to love these people easily, and I didn't want them to fail. It would be a big day.

We gathered in the plant a few minutes before the morning shift. They were on time. I stood on the elevated platform of a scissor jack. It was chilly. I'd been over the few words I would speak a hundred times since 4:00 a.m. As the platform ascended to a level about twenty-five feet above the plant floor, I looked out into the faces of several hundred wonderful souls, whom I knew had come to trust me. I was more than a little humbled. And more than a little scared.

As I went though my short sermon on cost reduction, which took no more than five minutes, what I saw was mostly furrowed brows, a plant-toughened hand cradling a bearded chin here and there. I saw a few husbands and wives, parents and kids and siblings standing together, listening intently with their shoulders touching. But there were no real signals. I ended, as I always did, with a recitation of our core values and of our purpose from vision. Everyone nodded in silent approval and turned to their stations. The shift bell sounded.

Back in my office I felt detached, like you sometimes do when you have a fever. What had just happened? Had I done the right thing? The only thing I knew was that those people would let me know, in their own way and in their own time. In my speech I'd asked them to give any ideas that they might have to their supervisors at the end of the shift, and that we'd go over whatever emerged in the next morning's operations meeting. I guessed that I'd just have to wait.

During the course of the day I spent about an hour and a half, as I usually did, on the plant floor. Still no signals. At the end of the shift I decided to walk out into the parking lot, as I also often did, to wave a few good-byes. My first thought was that I'd read my watch wrong. Pick-ups and cars weren't streaming for the gate. Confused, I made my way back to the plant. I'll never forget what I saw from the mezzanine catwalk.

Cells of crews were gathered in the free spaces everywhere, surrounding their supervisors like floor workers on the New York stock exchange, some even gesticulating wildly, while their harried leaders strove to maintain order while writing furiously on their yellow pads.

Wednesday's operations meeting lasted all day. Would this have happened seven months earlier? No. Were the ideas actionable? Effective? Some were not. But others were devastatingly so! I remember the flood of thankfulness that drowned me. Not for what had happened for me, but for them.

What needed to come next didn't take much thinking. In fact, it took none. We needed to reconfigure the senior management team, for a time, into a giant and enthusiastically grateful catcher's mitt. The last thing in the world I was going to do was to be unresponsive to this tsunami of mind, spirit, and soul.

So for a while we operated like a perennial ball club from the cellar that has an against-the-odds shot at a league pennant. There were lots of long nights for our management team and a few weekends together. We used mounds of chart paper and lots of pens. And we did lots of work in process feedback and clarification with our contributors. One conversation

I remember was with a recently hired laborer on the second shift. Chuckling, he observed to me that this was the first place he'd ever been where the office people worked for people in the plant. He was right. And that's how it ought to be in your business, too.

After several weeks of preparation, we had sorted through all the game films and were ready for our championship game. We'd also designed a process, a policy, and a control system for continuing to encourage and deal responsively with a less intense, but still consistent, flow of ideas for cost reduction. And we'd already begun to see the results in our metrics.

What I'd proven to myself, and what I now offer to you under the least likely of heading—cutting costs—is that running a company well requires a shift of thinking toward a life of service. Rather that hiding behind the awful reality of cutting jobs and reducing programs we believed were important, we took another route. We respected and trusted our people. We believed that the more noble thing was not to decide for them, but rather to recognize that they had insights that we'd never uncover. We asked them to join us in the solution. It worked for me then, and it's worked for me every time since. It will work for you. Even in territory as challenging as cost reduction.

How do we calibrate the impacts of solid Back of the Envelope, and Vision–Strategy–Execution thinking? How do we know if our commitments to fairness, integrity, respect, processes, policies, control systems, Kaizen, no-waste, safety, delivery, and cost are paying off? The answer lies partly in what you'll be feeling. But it's also in the numbers.

Let's go there.

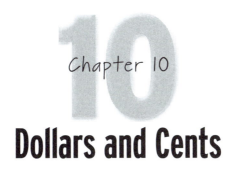

Chapter 10

Dollars and Cents

Though I should expect it by now, it still surprises me to find people with impeccable credentials in accounting and finance who are terrible at running their businesses. And on the other side, people who can't even balance their checkbooks may be great. Part of the incredulity comes, I believe, from our pervasive tendency to think of businesses primarily as number-generating entities, rather than social entities. The other clue from that observation is that what you need to know about numbers to do a pretty effective job of running a business isn't really all that difficult. In fact, I often see numbers-centric people overthinking their numbers, looking for all the right answers to rise from their spreadsheets and missing the fundamental points of their businesses.

So, what do you need to know about your numbers, particularly, if you aren't a financial jock? What's the right spin to put on your numbers to do an effective job of running your company?

Your Role in Managing the Money

I estimate that the U.S. workforce is divided about equally between people who are comfortable with numbers and people who aren't. And surprisingly, I've met just about as many who are great at running their businesses who are solidly anchored in the second category. That constitutes my thesis. You don't have to be a natural-born mathematician to manage the funds of your business and to manage them well. You just need to have enough interest in your business to understand how it works in a language that is different from, and actually much simpler than, words.

I often refer to managing funds as taking care of the arithmetic of a business, because arithmetic is the highest level of math required. There are no quadratic equations here. There's just adding, subtracting, dividing, and an occasional percentage or two.

I think of the three key funds management tools for businesses—the statement of profit and loss, the balance sheet, and the statement of cash flow—as telling the story of the past performance and of the current status of a business. Together, they answer a series of questions that anyone running a business should know in the same way that a ship's captain should know his vessel's position and its track at every moment in time:

How profitable has the business been?

How are the financial resources of the business currently deployed?

What's my risk of foreclosure?

To what degree has the business been generating or consuming money?

Where might I look to effect an improvement in financial performance?

Familiarity with the three key schedules is really all that's required to maintain your perspective on these questions most of the time. Of course, there are numerous other accounting schedules that generally become part of everyday life, things like accounts receivable aging schedules, depreciation schedules, bills of materials, routing schedules, inventory reports, freight rates, production reports, and the like. But with few exceptions, every one of them is either a back-up to, or a derivative of, one of the three key documents. Let's look at each one.

The Statement of Profit and Loss

The statement of profit and loss (P&L) tells the story of whether the business has created or lost profit over the period of time it measures, and gives important clues as to the reasons for the result. Most businesses produce a P&L on a monthly, a quarterly, and an annual basis. It is usually divided into three sections with important, but simply calculated, subtotals bridging each one, and leading up to a summary of overall profitability, called profit after tax, or net income, at the bottom.

Revenues	$10,000
Less: Discounts and Allowances	(500)
Total Revenues	9,500
Cost of Goods Sold	6,500
Gross Margin	3,000
Period Costs	2,000
Profit before Tax	1,000
Tax	280
Profit After Tax	$720

The first section outlines the sources of revenues and usually also includes any offsets to revenues, such as discounts and allowances that might include price reductions on certain orders to reflect special circumstances. The numbers in this section are summarized in a simple subtotal, usually called total revenues, which indicates the inflow of funds for the period of the statement.

The next section documents the costs of the labor, materials, and other consumables that were used up in the production of the goods or services that were sold during the period. These costs are recorded as they are incurred, and not necessarily as they are paid. The idea here is to match costs with the revenues in the period when the revenues were recorded.

Also included in this section is an estimate of the value of the nonconsumable, fixed items—like the plant and equipment—that, theoretically, were used up gradually, in addition to the consumables, to produce the goods or services that generated the revenues in the period. The specification of this consumption of fixed costs is accomplished by estimating the useful life of the item in question then applying a pro rata share of its original cost, sometimes according to an accelerated schedule, to the period. The subtotal of the numbers in this section is customarily called cost of goods, or services, sold. The result of subtracting the cost of goods or services sold from the subtotal of the first section, total revenues, yields one of the numbers that anyone running a business should be mindful of every minute of every day. This is the gross margin.

The gross margin is the amount of funds left over from revenues after the costs of goods or services sold for the period have been incurred. Gross margin, therefore, is the amount of funds available to cover all the other costs over the period of the statement and, hopefully, leave a profit. Gross margin is customarily expressed both as an absolute number and as a percentage of period revenues on the statement.

Gross margin is a hugely important number. Though simple in its construct, I believe that most of the time, except in times of financial crisis, it is the single most important number in your business. It lets you know the level of all of the other costs that the business can afford. When there's an excess, it indicates that you have funds to invest to grow your business. When there's a shortfall, it telegraphs the message that the business either has to increase revenues through greater sales volumes or higher pricing, or to cut costs quickly in order to remain solvent. Even slight variations in its percentage of cost of goods sold can drive extraordinary changes in the overall profitability of the enterprise.

Most people I talk with about managing the funds of their businesses tell me that they pay the most attention, when they receive their new P&Ls, to their revenues. Maybe it's because revenues are at the top of the page. My attention, however, is always riveted on gross margin, which usually appears in the middle of the statement. Looking up the schedule from gross margin, I want to see how changes in revenues have been reflected in the gross margin. Due to the existence of fixed costs, variations in revenues will have an effect on gross margin as a percentage. Here, I often also do a side calculation to neutralize the effect of volume and isolate the degree to which consumables have been turned into gross margin funds for the period for each of the major categories of cost of goods sold. Then, looking down the schedule, I want to know whether the amount of gross margin is sufficient to cover the period costs.

The next section of the P&L contains the description of the period costs. These should include all of the nonproduction–related costs of the business, with the exception of taxes. All of the support functions—sales, marketing, accounting, business insurance, administration, and the like—reside here. The downfall of most businesses is in their failure to adjust the period costs to shortfalls in gross margin. If total revenues do not materialize as planned and gross margin dollars follow suit, period costs must be reduced accordingly, and quickly. If you don't have a solid and immediately action-able idea for how to improve the gross margin situation—by increasing revenues or lowering costs of goods or services sold—you need to reduce the period costs. Reduce them more than the amount needed to bring the current situation into balance, because it will take you a while to have your solution effectively in place. And things seldom get better in the interim.

Bringing period costs in line is usually the toughest thing that a person running a business has to do, because it typically means reducing people or amenities that everyone has grown accustomed to having. If you find yourself having difficulty doing this, if you find yourself procrastinating and hoping that the next statement will yield more promising results, you are in the company of many people running businesses. But it might be best to either seek strong, pragmatic guidance or to turn the reins over to someone else. This sounds harsh, but the inability to match period costs with the realities of gross margin is the root of business decline that I see most frequently. At a recent conference of the collision repair business I ran, one of our franchisees tearfully told the story of how he asked his mom to resign her post so that he would be able to pay his other workers through a particularly tough time. Five hundred people stood and applauded. Most wished that they, too, had the courage of that young body shop owner in St. Louis.

Subtracting the period costs from the gross margin yields operating income, often called profit or earnings before taxes (PBT or EBT). Though a big focus for many, particularly bankers, it is a number in the P&L that really doesn't mean that much to me. Its major significance is to give me an idea of how much the business can afford to pay for costs associated with its tax obligations, and leave an acceptable profit for the ownership.

Below PBT are the tax obligations that the business incurred but did not necessarily pay during the period, which are subtracted from PBT to get profit after tax, or net income.

In summary, looking at the P&L as a whole I want to know:

Is the gross margin sufficient? Is it improving? Declining?

> If it's not sufficient or improving, what are the most likely and achievable solutions? Greater sales volume? Higher prices? Lower costs of goods or services?

Are the period costs aligned with realistic gross margin expectations?

> How much more revenue volume could the business support without adding to period costs? If the answer is a significant number, I either want to quickly grow revenues to that number, or reduce the period costs. Not later. Now.
> If the gross margin looks insufficient and I am unsure about whether and how I might improve it, I want to reduce the period costs. Now.
> Alternatively, if I could add to period costs and get a greater, or parallel, increase in gross margin dollars, such as increasing revenues by adding a salesperson, or reducing costs of goods by adding a machine, I should do it.

Is the profit margin acceptable?

> If it's not, I've got three places to look for fixes. Can I (1) increase revenues, (2) reduce costs of goods sold, or (3) reduce period costs to generate an acceptable level of profitability? Ninety percent of the time the answer here is yes, and often yes in more than one place—if the person in charge of running the business is willing to recognize that imperative and act on it.

There is a strong message in this 90 percent prediction: Few businesses, regardless of their current financial performance, don't realize an enterprise could be more profitable if it were the entire focus of management's attention and allocation of funds.

But, in many instances it takes an unusual ability to distance one's self from familiarity and comfort with the current circumstances, along with a considerable measure of courage, to view such an alternative as an opportunity. It can mean dramatically downsizing for a while. It can mean undoing things that have served the business well for years. It can mean trauma for a lot of people, including your investors and banker. It can mean calling an end to the charade that things will get better on their own. And that's why so few people are able to do it. Rather than initiate and then endure the discomfort of a painful but effective fix, they choose "death by a thousand cuts," sliding down the latter half of the product life cycle into decline.

But you shouldn't be one of those people. And maniacal attention to your periodic statements of profit and loss will give you the perspective and all the signals you need to avoid that outcome. The rest is up to you.

The Balance Sheet

When I was in business school, we were all taught that the balance sheet is a "snapshot of the business at a point in time." It was one of those blind mantras, so pervasive that no one even thought about questioning whether it made sense. In my own case, I think I understood what they were saying, in a general way, but it never really meant quite as much to me as it seemed to mean to the accounting faculty. And I always wished that it did.

Yes, I understood that the P&L describes performance of the business over a period of time and that the balance sheet is a description of assets and liabilities at one particular point in time, but it took a few years of working with the concepts for me to find a better way of thinking about the balance sheet. I did eventually figure out a way that meant more to me, and I hope that it means more to you.

Today, I think of the balance sheet not as a snapshot, but rather as an important part of a story. It tells me how the business has assembled and deployed its financial resources up to the date of the schedule. And the P&L shows me what the results have been. In a sense the two statements document the story of an experiment. What was tried—the balance sheet—and the result—the P&L. These two statements make a lot of sense to me when viewed in this way. Together, they give me a complete picture, through numbers and from a financial point of view, of how the business has been run and with what degree of success.

Assets		*Liabilities*	
Current Assets		Current Liabilities	
Cash	$500	Payables	$2,000
Near Cash Assets	500	Long-Term Liabilities	
Receivables	1,500	Bank Loan	5,000
Inventory	900	Family Loan	1,000
Total Current Assets	3,400	Total Liabilities	8,000
Fixed Assets		Owner's Equity	
Plant & Equipment	3,500	Stock at Par Value	500
Vehicles	3,500	Additional Paid In	1,500
Other	500	Retained Earnings	900
Total Fixed Assets	7,500	Total Equity	2,900
Total Assets	$10,900	Total Liabilities and Equity	$10,900

Most businesses produce a balance sheet whenever they produce a P&L. It's divided vertically into a right and a left side. The right side of the balance sheet shows where the funds deployed in the business have come from. The top half of the right side shows the funds that the business has gotten from others free, usually in the form of payment terms that have been extended from suppliers. You have received their supplies but have not yet had to pay for them, and they are not charging you interest in the interim.

The next lower section on the right side reveals the sources of funds that the business is paying for—its various forms of long-term debt. The costs associated with this debt show up on the P&L as interest charges.

The summation of the current liabilities and long-term debt sections is called total liabilities, and it represents the amount of money that would be owed to creditors if the business were terminated on the day that the balance sheet was produced.

Below total liabilities, at the bottom of the right side, is the equity section, which I'll come back to after we talk about the left side of the balance sheet.

The left side of the balance sheet shows how the funds from the right side have been and are being used, as of the date of the balance sheet. The first entry on the left-hand side is cash. This shows the bank account balances on the date of the statement. Right below cash, there might be another entry for near-cash assets, like marketable securities, things that could be readily converted into cash if required.

The section below cash, called receivables, shows the amount of funds that the business is owed by others and expects to collect, generally within ninety days, but has not yet received. Receivables result either from invoices that have been sent to customers for goods or services delivered but not yet collected, or from short-term notes, such as an employee advance on pay. This section also shows any allocations of funds to prepaids. Prepaids are expenditures that the business has made for mostly nontangible consumables, like association memberships or insurance policies, that are expected to be used up over the relatively near-term future, through the course of normal operations.

The next section down is inventories. The inventories section is usually subdivided into three categories. The first summarizes the value of things, like raw materials, parts, coatings, and packaging that the business has acquired, but has not yet begun to use, for the production of goods and services. The second category, generally called work in progress, includes the value of inventory that is caught in the process of being converted, but not yet converted, to final outputs on the date of the statement. The third category indicates the value of finished goods that have not yet been sold and shipped to customers.

The values for all three categories are shown at the lower of original cost or current market value. If there are items still on hand that were purchased at prices lower than they could be resold for today, the inventory numbers will under-represent the true value of the goods on hand. Unfortunately, the reverse is more frequently the case. I often find inventories on the balance sheets of businesses that should have been "written down"—restated at a lower value—to reflect their obsolescence or reduced values in the market-place. Why haven't these companies reduced the values of their inventories on their balance sheets to reflect changed realities? Because, as we shall see shortly, such actions reduce reported profitability, which reduces the value of the enterprise along with the value of the shareholders' equity.

The last section describes the more permanent things that have been acquired to support the business, typically plant, equipment, intellectual property, and the like, again at the lower of cost or current market value, and net of depreciation. Depreciation is the concept used to estimate the declining value of a long-term asset as it is used up over its lifetime. It is a calculation that divides the original cost of the item by its useful life, esti-mated at the time of its acquisition. The resulting amount is added, period by period over the useful life of the item as an expense on the P&L, and is deducted correspondingly period to period from the original cost of the item on the balance sheet. Within the limits of the tax code, the deprecia-tion of most assets and the associated charges that are transferred over to the P&L can be accelerated. Real estate is an exception. Accelerating the schedule of depreciation of an asset has the effect of reducing pre-tax prof-its reported on the P&L, but carries the attendant benefits of reducing tax payments during the period and of increasing cash.

I want to add one caution here. The attention that some people pay to managing the balance sheet to avoid or to delay paying taxes can be misleading to some mainstream business owners. Why? First, because the near-term effect of a tax deferral, but not a credit, may be reversed and recaptured in the later years of an asset's life. And second, because these practices distort the reality of the financial performance of your actual operations, and you need to know, every minute of the journey, just where you stand. As a person running a mainstream private business, I must have accurate knowledge of what my real operating costs and profits are for a period of time and what they have been. If I choose to distort these numbers to create a more favorable tax position, I've also got to see the other side. You do not want to be misled about the financial risk position, or of the true earning potential, of your business. And if you are not capable of translating the accounting statements generated for tax purposes into accurate reflections of what's actually going on in your business, get help from someone who can.

Returning to the balance sheet, the sum of the top and bottom halves of the left side is labeled total assets—it's a combination of the depreciated cost and market values of all of the things that have been acquired to run the business.

Back on the right side of the balance sheet, and more specifically in the section just below the total liabilities summary, we'll find the final, and the most interesting, part of the balance sheet. This is the shareholder equity section. Like the gross margin line on the P&L, the shareholders equity line is the first place I look on the balance sheet.

There are usually two key numbers for me in this section. The first is the amount that investors—yourself, family, and friends if your business is private, or people you don't even know if your business is publicly traded—have contributed to the business in return for stock ownership. Usually, this amount is shown as the sum of two sub-items that are entitled (1) common stock at par and (2) capital paid in excess of par. The sum of the two is the cumulative value of all of the funds that have been invested by shareholders, either public or private, posted at their original investment values. If, for example, an unknown investor, or your brother, bought 100 shares five years ago at $5.00 per share, with a par value of ten cents per share, the entries here would be:

Common Stock at Par	10.00
Capital Paid in Excess of Par	490.00
Total Stock	$500.00

The second key number in this section is cumulative retained earnings. This is the current running total of the profits and losses that the business has recorded since its inception, minus the cumulative value of earnings that have been distributed as dividends. In most statements, the current month's earnings are shown separately and correspond to the same net income number shown on the P&L. If cumulative earnings is a positive number, the business has generated a positive return on investors' investment, in excess of any dividends that might have been paid out to them along the way. If it's negative, it's likely that your shareholders' wealth has been eroded by their investment in your business.

The summary of what investors have invested in return for stock coupled with the cumulative earnings that have been posted over time equals shareholder equity, which also equals the difference between the total assets on the left side of the balance sheet and the total liabilities, shown on the right, in the section immediately above.

Shareholder equity represents the amount of value that is assignable to the owners of the business as returns for committing their money to ownership positions in the business. It also shows the value of what should be left over, if the valuations of assets are accuate on the statement, and distributable to the shareholders, if the business were terminated on the date of the balance sheet, after all liabilities were paid off. But the most useful way for me to think about shareholders' equity is that it shows, from an accounting point of view, how good an investment the business has been for its shareholders.

Most of the time I look at the balance sheet after I've looked at the P&L—though most audited financial statements package them in the reverse order—and I am looking for three things:

To what degree is the business vulnerable to being forced into insolvency by its creditors?

To what degree does it have the capacity to fund its future?

To what degree has it been a good investment for its shareholders?

A comparison of the assets with the liabilities usually answers the first two questions, and a look at the shareholders' equity section answers the third.

The Statement of Cash Flow

Largely because of the existence of noncash items in the P&L, like depreciation expenses for tangible long-term assets and accrual charges for amortizations of intangible long-term assets, profit after tax is not accurate as a picture of the degree to which cash has actually been accumulated or depleted during the period of the P&L. There are several simple adjustments to the P&L that convert it into a better approximation of the cash dynamics of the period, but I prefer an entirely different schedule here. The statement of cash flow ties back to the cash balances in the business bank accounts and gives the person in charge what I believe is the most reliable outlook on the funds that she has, and likely will have, over the near term, to pay the obligations of the enterprise.

This statement of cash flow starts with the current balances in the bank accounts. Your financial person ought to know these at all times. If you don't have a financial person, just call the bank. Next, I add the near-term receivables—the amount that is, or will be, owed to the business and that is expected to be collected before the next requirement for a major payout, usually the next payroll or repayment of debt. Then, I record as negative numbers the total of the checks that have been issued by the business but not yet processed—those that have not yet cleared the bank account—and any automatic or manual withdrawals that will be made during the period before the next major payment. I label the sum of these numbers available funds. This number tells me how much money I should have to run the business over the next increment of time, in this case until the next payroll.

Then I turn to the bills that I expect to have to pay over the same upcoming period. Usually, I simply ask for a summary of the payables register for the same timeframe and record the total as a negative number. Finally, I also add any other payments that I know about, but that might not be recorded in the payables register, as negative numbers. This might include things like prepayments or amounts that I know might be needed to resolve an unplanned event, like a threatened lawsuit.

In the last step, I summarize the string of numbers and compare it to the amount I expect to have to lay out to cover the next major expenditure, in this case the next payroll. Hopefully, the calculation result exceeds the expenditure value by a comfortable margin. If not, I've got early warning of the need to begin conserving, or seeking an infusion of, cash.

Often I'll extend this exercise out over three months on an Excel spreadsheet and review and update it weekly. It always surprises me how many times people running businesses find themselves surprised by a cash shortfall crisis. Do this every week and you won't be one of them.

Valuation

There's a lot of talk these days about business valuation. Most people seem to agree that the purpose of a business is to create value. At least they say it frequently. But a lot of people don't really understand how valuation is calculated or monitored, or what they might be able to do, in addition to running their businesses as they have in the past, to affect it.

The roots of thinking about valuation come out of the appraisal profession. Traditionally, business appraisers looked to the intersection of three separate kinds of analyses in order to calculate the value of a business. The first was replacement cost. How much would it cost, starting from scratch, to build a business comparable to the one under scrutiny. The second angle was liquidation value, often called adjusted book value. How much would be distributable to the shareholders after all the debts were paid off if the business were simply shut down? This is different from the shareholder equity shown on the accounting statements because it includes the current market value of the assets—versus the lower of cost or book value reflected in the accounting statements—and it recognizes and includes the value of intangibles such as a brand name, proprietary technology, or unique market position that someone might pay extra to acquire.

Over time, however, the third approach has generally become the standard for most valuation exercises. This one has to do with pegging the current value of a business to an assessment of its potential for future cash generation. The theory here is that if one can project the future distributable cash that a business is likely to generate over, say, the next three to five years, before the costs for interest and taxes are taken out, and if one can assign a level of risk to that likelihood, then one should be able to determine how much a person (or entity) would be willing to pay in order to own the rights to the prospect of that future cash stream.

Accountants call this a discounted cash flow analysis. The adjective "discounted" refers to a deduction that is factored into the calculation to account for two things. The first is the interest income opportunity that would be foregone by investing funds in the business, versus investing the funds in a relatively "risk free" instrument. The second is an interest rate "kicker" that accounts for the additional risk that the investor associates with a prospective investment in the business, versus a "risk free" instrument. The riskier the outlook, the higher the "kicker" needs to be in order to entice someone into the investment, and hence, the lower the valuation. It's really not much different from betting on anything else. The lower the odds are of winning, the higher the payoff needs to be to get people to put their money on the line.

The "risk free" opportunity cost of funds is fairly easy to estimate. It is usually taken as the return one would get on a Treasury note for a comparable period of time. To illustrate, if funds were not used to purchase the business, they could be invested in Treasury notes for the same period of time that would deliver a published rate of return on a largely "risk free" basis. So, anyone thinking about buying a business should expect to get a return on the price they are paying that is equal, at a bare minimum, to the return they would expect if they bought a largely "risk free" Treasury note for a time period comparable to the time they think they will be committing their money to the business.

But nearly every business is riskier than a treasury investment. And the level of that risk needs to be reflected in the premium, above the "risk free" return that the purchaser needs to believe that he or she can achieve through ownership of the business in order make the investment. The sum of the "risk free" return and this premium is called the risk-adjusted required rate of return. In other words, it's the rate of return that a prudent investor would require, taking into account his assessment of the risks associated with the future cash generation of a specific business, in order to make the deal.

Fortunately, there is a starting point for calculating the risk-adjusted required rate of return for investments in businesses, just as there is for the "risk free." It's based on the long-term returns that people have enjoyed from investments in public securities. Most analysts agree that the returns over the long term to investments in publicly traded equities, stock, have averaged around 9 percent. And this is a starting point. If you feel that the business in question is no more or no less risky than an investment in an average equity security, the appropriate risk-adjusted required rate of return would be 9 percent.

Another, and simpler, way of taking into account the risk associated with a business investment is as a cash flow multiplier, versus a discount rate, and nearly everybody does it this way these days. The calculation is infinitely easier than discount arithmetic and is close enough for nearly all valuation purposes up to serious deal making, where analysis of discounted cash flows usually comes back into play. The conversion goes like this.

Let's say you come up with a risk-adjusted required rate of return of 12 percent on an investment that yielded $120,000 of cash flow over the last twelve months, and this rate of return is expected to continue over the next ten years. The fairly cumbersome discounted cash flow calculation yields a value, called by the accountants a discounted present value, of this cash stream with this risk of $678,000. Dividing the valuation by the annual cash flow yields a number, the valuation multiplier of 5.65x, which can be applied to the cash flow—5.65 × $120,000 = $678,000—to get the value. It's a lot easier this way.

Typically, the valuation multiplier on average businesses runs in the range of four to six times the cash flow. Riskier businesses will have lower valuation multipliers. For those with lower risk and higher prospects for future cash flow, the valuation multiples are higher.

Where things get illogical are in the valuations of businesses with little or no earnings, but with great prospects. During tech bubbles, multiples of a hundred or higher are talked about, based on future expectations for cash flow that are monumental leaps from historical performance. With such scant connection to any observable reality, the cash flow multiple approach to valuation loses credibility quickly, and the prices in these situations usually wind up being determined not by any rational approach to valuation but rather according to who will pay the most to gain control of the hype surrounding the business that's being sold.

Thinking about the Value of Your Company

Assuming that you are not running an emerging technology business but one with a history of earnings and cash flow and without a lot of wild hype surrounding its future, the best place to start thinking about the valuation of your own business is to find out what multipliers other businesses like yours have brought in recent transactions. Through a number of online services that monitor mergers and acquisitions, you can find summaries of transactions of both publicly traded and private companies in just about any industry you can imagine. CEOs interested in the value of their own enterprises can, and should, keep close tabs on recent transactions in their industries and among their near-industry counterparts.

Once you have zeroed in on a reasonable multiplier for transactions involving businesses like yours, your next challenge is to project your own cash flow. In cash flow, like lots of things, most people believe that a first step toward understanding the future is to understand the past. Often, people in business talk about LTM. This means cash generation over the last twelve months, and it's become almost a ubiquitous and foundational notion in business valuation. Your own LTM is usually easy enough to calculate from your business's financial statements. It's another number that any responsible CEO or president needs to understand and be aware of continuously. If you don't know it, here's how to get there.

Your LTM income statement will end with a number called net income after tax. This number usually includes a number of cost items, like depreciation of equipment and amortization of intangible items like research and development, which do not require actual expenditures of cash. So these non-cash expense items and any others like them from your P&L need to be added back to your net income after tax, to begin getting back to cash flow. Also, because an acquirer will be bringing his own financing to a transaction and wants to know how much cash will be available to service its own capital structure, and because paying off the long-term debt of the company with the proceeds of the sale will be in most instances your responsibility, any costs for interest should also be added back. And finally, because tax strategies will vary from one prospective owner to another, and because any prospective new owner also will want to know how much he can count on being available to cover future taxes, costs for taxes also are added back.

Your approximation of cash flow for your LTM accounting period, therefore, will be:

Net Income After Taxes + Interest Costs + Taxes Paid + Depreciation + Amortization.

This calculation is referred to as EBITDA—Earnings before Interest, Taxes, Depreciation, and Amortization. It is the universal, accepted estimate of cash flow for business valuation purposes.

The application of your multiplier to your estimate of EBITDA, then, gives you an estimate of the value of your business. In cases where you believe that the future cash flows from your business won't be stable, but rather will be increasing or decreasing annually, you have two choices. One, you can interpolate and negotiate about what annual number best represents the average expectation. Or two, you can revert to the discounted cash flow calculation that incorporates the flexibility to account for annual fluctuations in cash flow expectations.

Now for some other considerations. Typically, there is a valuation deduction that reflects the unavailability of a ready market—like a stock exchange—for ownership interests in nonpublic and closely held businesses. This often turns out to be a fraction of a multiple point or up to a few multiple points, depending on how esoteric your business is. For an independent grocery store that is a ready target for acquisition by a chain, the deduction might be zero. For a privately held manufacturer of vintage sewing machine parts, however, the deduction might be a half or more of the multiple before consideration of the deduction.

On the other hand, valuable intellectual property, such as patents, trademarks, or powerful brands, which might have value beyond their current applications in the business under its current ownership, might bring a premium over either the discounted cash flow or multiple approach to valuation.

Similarly, profitable, long-term contracts with customers or partnering agreements that raise the switching costs for customers will add to valuation. And finally, things that need to be fixed or upgraded—typically roofs, mechanical systems, production equipment, vehicles, computers, and software systems—will result in deductions.

So, how do you maximize the value of your business? The rules are pretty simple:

Maximize your current cash flow and EBITDA.

Create a believable story for business growth and greater cash flows going forward.

Reduce the perception of risk associated with your performance through things like steady historical earnings, freedom from dependence on major customers, low cost position, and technological parity with your competitors.

Build a strong and committed management team that is capable of maintaining the performance of the business without you.

Maintain plant, equipment, and systems in serviceable condition.

Develop a defensible uniqueness through things like proprietary technology, superior service, long-term contracts with customers, and branding.

Pay off debt.

The point I've made throughout this chapter is that you don't need to be a financial wizard to be a competent manager of your company's funds and to maximize its value. If you can carry with you the ideas of the Back of the Envelope and the Vision–Strategy–Execution frameworks, the concept of renewal as a way of life, and a commitment to leadership and management of people and funds, you can be confident you are pursuing the right course. How far you can go depends on how well you can integrate into your leadership style the material in the next chapter. If the thoughts resonate, you're on your way to greatness. Best of luck. The world needs more of you.

Chapter 11

Love and Business, and Other Important Things

This has been the most challenging chapter of this book to write. It's also been the most challenging to think about. But it is also the one I feel most certain about. And it is, clearly, the most important.

It took more than a decade and a half for me to distill a number of strongly felt, but at the time only vaguely defined, impressions into ideas I could articulate. Once these ideas began to take form for me, however, they proceeded rapidly and became blindingly and unalterably requisite in my own thinking about how to run businesses. Today, I simply can't separate the concepts outlined in the chapters up to this point from the thoughts I am about to share.

Your understanding of what's in these next few pages will do more than anything that's come before to support you in running your company responsibly. Everything I've talked about up to this point has proven enormously useful in helping people do the noble job of running businesses well. But what you are about to read now adds the depth, the luminescence, the attraction, and the vibrancy to these more pragmatic concepts. It helps you to turn your knowledge of running businesses into lasting and meaningful contributions to other people's lives, and to your own.

With the logic and a framework for running a business now in place, I can talk about the spirit that you carry with you when you use them to do your work. Know that your motives and your attitudes underpin everything you do in your job. The spirit with which you infuse your work is what people will remember most about you, and it's what will endure long after you, in fact, are gone and your voice and your face are forgotten.

This chapter is not like those that have come before. Those chapters have been about what you should do. This chapter is about how you should be while you are carrying out your plans. More specifically, it's about the portion of how that is anchored in why. It's about the reason that the people who are most successful at running companies want to do it. Because why they want to do it lies at the root of their ability to engender loyalty and followership, and to be successful according to all the other measures of success.

This chapter is about love. Love in the humanitarian sense. It's not the blindingly infatuating, heart-pounding, scream-your-head-off, paint-her-name-on-the-water-tower kind, which tends to be fleeting. The kind of love I am talking about is the quiet, slowly moving, rock-solid, dependable, reverent, metamorphosed-over-time kind, the kind that tends to endure.

This sense about yourself and about your relations to others is rooted in an understanding about your purpose for living that I believe comes to everyone, eventually. It comes to some earlier and easier than to others. Some may not get it until their last breath. But because nobody talks about it much, particularly in businesses, where we spend so much of our lives, it generally comes to most of us later than when we first need it. Usually it comes through our reflections about seemingly important things in our lives that haven't worked out as well as we'd hoped. Life has a way of honing us more effectively through our failures than through our successes. And it has a way of giving all of us plenty of failures to work with. As proof, I can say that most of the people I know who are the best at running their businesses have come to learn what's in this chapter the hard way.

Love, even the kind that's relevant here, is sometimes difficult to talk about without getting wound up in religion, or in a more formal discussion of peoples' faith. Granted, religion and faith are mostly about love, and many of our ideas about the kind of love I'm talking about come from religious thinking and writings. But this is not a book about religion or faith, so I'm avoiding that angle. Nonetheless, one of the best and most relevant treatises I've ever read about the role of love in all aspects of our lives has its roots in the idea of spiritual living, in a broadly defined and nonsectarian way, and I have yet to find a better approach for explaining the concept.

Henry Drummond, a Scotsman, was a widely regarded nineteenth-century scientist and religious scholar. From his posts at the University of Edinburgh and later in Glasgow, he developed a following of people who carried his thinking to many far-flung places on the globe. About ten years ago, a very dear friend gave me a reprint of a lecture that Professor Drummond delivered in 1883 to a missionary outpost in Central Africa entitled, "The Greatest Thing in the World." Reading it left me dumbfounded. Nearly a hundred and twenty years earlier, Drummond had penned the elegant solution to a problem that I had worked on for years, and it had been right under my nose.

Since then, I've read the lecture at least two hundred times. I've read it so frequently that I have a hard time now remembering the way I thought before I read it, versus the way I think now. Accordingly, the remainder of this chapter contains at its core much of Professor Drummond's thinking; its application to the running of businesses is my contribution.

When I was in business school, most of us thought about running a company as the ultimate, the pinnacle, of job achievement. For those of us who got the chance, it would be "the greatest job in the world." Wrapped up in that goal was the opportunity to realize in our lives at work a complex mixture of other aspirations that included responsibility, authority, power, prestige, fame, wealth, security, independence, and control. Also, and I believe underlying virtually all of our other aspirations, we shared an idealistic yearning to someday be free from fear—free from the fear of never attaining control over our own destinies at work, and thereby having the chance, instead of working for someone else, to demonstrate our own full potentials in making decisions and directing the work of others.

Our desire to run a business, then, was really all about breaking away from a life of dependence, the kind of dependence we'd nearly all been incredibly blessed with since birth and were continuing to enjoy as our parents paid for tuition. The frequent stories about those who'd reached the pinnacle and failed miserably never seemed to register on our screens. Such was the allure. For us, it was all about getting our chance at the gold ring, and about the glorious freedom to which it would lead.

Running a business was our definition of "the good life," the ultimate achievement, as I believe it still is for many. But, I believe that this youthful aspiration also spells doom for those who get to the top with "the good life" still intact as their major motivation. This misguided aspiration is why so few who grab the gold ring truly succeed. It is why there are so few who are really good at running businesses. And because of the pervasive influence that the character and performance of the person at the top of the organization has on other peoples' lives, it's the reason there are so few people whose time at work—where they spend the majority of their waking hours—is truly a blessing. For all too many, work is, at its worst, a source of anguish, or more frequently, a requisite annoyance in their lives.

Invariably, I've found that those rare individuals who have the gift of making life at work different do it from a wholly different platform than the one most people think about when aspiring to run a business. For those gifted few, running a business is not about self-achievement, self-fulfillment, or self-actualization. They don't go to work thinking about what they're going to get done that day or about who they're going to impress.

Rather, what's on their minds all the time is what everyone else is going to get done, and very importantly, how everyone else is going to feel about the day when they get home. It's not that they aren't realists. Nor do these really successful leaders and managers always see their jobs in a rosy glow. It's just the opposite. If a leader truly loves and respects her colleagues, it is her responsibility to give them the truth and nothing but the truth, but to do it from a platform of unusual understanding about what it means to believe in them, and to love them.

In 1883, Drummond recounted for all of us how to build this philosophy into all aspects of our lives, and thereby to create for ourselves what he called the summum bonum, translated the "supreme good." For me, an important point is that Drummond presented his thoughts clearly as a recounting, and not as his original ideas. What he wrote didn't spring from a unique revelation that came to him alone; rather, he related his treatise to ancient principles for living the supreme good life, themes that have been part of responsible thinking about the way that nature works since the beginning of time. Drummond simply recalled these ideas for his audience in Central Africa, and for me as well, in a way that is a kind and powerful reminder of something we always knew, but that we should be trying harder to carry in our consciousness every day.

In much the way that a seasoned and educated painter might start a new canvas by sketching the composition of one of the great artworks of the past, Drummond begins his lecture with a familiar passage of the New Testament of the Bible. This short passage gives the apostle Paul's synopsis for the citizens of Corinth of all of the knowledge and wisdom that had preceded him on the substance of a good life. This is the framework for the summum bonum from Drummond, with guidelines on how to live it. It includes nine keystones, not only for your own good life, but also, I believe, for your success in running businesses and, therefore, for your capacity to contribute to the good lives of others.

These nine keys are: patience, kindness, generosity, humility, courtesy, unselfishness, good humor, guilelessness, and sincerity. This is certainly not the stuff we talked about in business school. And they're not the kinds of traits we normally think about when we think of acting like a big-shot CEO (most of whom eventually fail and which, I believe, further supports my point).

Ask people who have been in the presence of a continually successful business leader, a leader who has accomplished things that others thought impossible, what it was like to be with him. They will tell you that there was something special about that person, something that they can't quite put their finger on, but definitely something special. I've been through that exercise more than anyone else I know, and I believe that the something special is the rare and innate understanding that those people have of the following principles.

Patience

One of the better-selling business books of the last few decades was about the strategic significance of speed. In today's "I want it now" culture, in order to be optimally competitive a business needs to be first to market with new ideas, first to offer the shortest order cycles, and first to have the shortest plant throughputs and the shortest delivery times in order to beat the competition. Who can argue with that idea? Where, then, does the virtue of, or even a modest tolerance for, patience possibly fit in? The answer lies in being able to separate, intellectually, two very similar but distinct perspectives on patience. One is about the mission of your business, with its attendant strategy and execution plans. The other is about the people upon whom you are, and will be, relying to get it done.

With regard to the first idea, your mission and its achievement, I've always been a proponent of high impatience and of stretch goals. If you think you might get to $5 million in sales, set your goal at $6. If you think it'll take a year to accomplish your mission, set the finish line at nine months. The Kaizen experience proves that we often have the capacity to do much better than we think we can.

But while there are a few people running businesses who always seem to achieve these kinds of stretch goals, most of the others don't. What's the difference? I believe it lies in how well the achievers understand and deal with the second idea, which is about the people who have to make it happen.

Similar to the Theory of Constraints, in which boundaries free people to exercise their creative freedom, my own Theory of Patience asserts that the best way to get people to go fast is to let them know why there is a need to go fast, and then to be encouraging and patient with their progress. How many times have you been exhorted by a boss or a coach who rants and raves about what needs to happen by when, "Or else!" More frequently, I venture, than you like to remember. And how often did the ranting and raving achieve the intended result? Less frequently, I venture, than the ranters like to remember.

And that shouldn't be much of a surprise. It's a pattern we've all learned to follow since childhood. People, including kids, don't like to be threatened. Threaten me and I'll resist. Spank me, ground me, reprimand me, put a letter in my file, demote me, and you'll fail in changing my attitude. In fact, you'll increase my resolve not to comply with whatever it is that you want. Physically, you might overpower me, but you'll never get me to do any more than the minimum required to survive while supporting your intention. Great organizational accomplishments don't accrue to minimum compliance efforts.

If, on the other hand, people like how you treat them, believe that you believe in them, understand what needs to get accomplished and understand why it's important—they'll generally reach the goal, if it's possible to be reached. The key is in getting them to want to help you, and a big factor here is whether or not you (1) exhibit an understanding of what's possible, (2) care about them, and (3) are willing to accept the absolute best that they can deliver in helping you achieve your intended end. Given that set of circumstances, most people will give you their total and unreserved all.

On the other hand, there's not much that's more demotivating than feeling that you are trying your best but that you are letting someone down. Most of us have been there. No matter what you do, it's just not good enough. Soon, you conclude that overexertion is not worth the effort. It's not appreciated and it's pointless. Then, if the pressure continues, a sick sense of enjoyment might even arise, derived from watching your exhorter fail, even if you are included in the consequences.

By contrast, there's nothing much more motivating than the prospect of amazing someone who cares about you. It's the highest joy of accomplishment. And who is it that we generally care about most? That's easy. It's whomever we believe believes in us most. These are the last people we are willing to disappoint: our moms, our favorite teachers, our best friends, our most inspiring bosses. They are the ones to whom we give our all. This willingness to sacrifice for the ones who believe in us most is why men do selfless and unthinkable things in the heat of battle. They perform heroic feats so that they don't let down the person who believes in them—the guy in the same foxhole, the guy who understands better than anyone else in the world the hopes, fears, and terrors they both are experiencing, and who looks to his buddy at his side for confidence and strength. You will not let that man down.

Which gets us back to patience. Patience is an extraordinary way of letting people know that you care about them. Your recognition that your employees are doing their best and your confidence that they will accomplish the seemingly impossible task is, I believe, an amphetamine for the spirit. Through your patience and through your genuine confidence in them, people will find ways to do things that will amaze everyone, including themselves.

Stated differently, my Theory of Patience is, "Go Slow to Go Fast." A burst of speed that saps both the physical and emotional energy of your team is not worth the effort, because it's not sustainable. Speed that builds gradually, which forgives mistakes along the way, and which allows well-motivated people to figure out for themselves how to maximize their potential, lasts and continues to deliver benefits over time.

How about times when neither the desired effect nor even weak signals of it are forthcoming? How does patience work then? Well, there are limits. But before reaching an ultimate limit, there can be milestones along the way. I call them "gut checks." They are where everyone who has signed up to a commitment gets together to "fold in" what they've learned since making the commitment, and to reassess do-ability, timing, resource requirements, and so on. What's different about these events is that you participate, not just as the guy who waves around the previous "lay across the tracks" commitments that people have made, but as a team member, as a thinker, and as part of the solution.

Your introduction to such a gathering might be something along the lines of, "Here we are at our first milestone 'gut check' and we're clearly behind where we all thought we'd be according to our schedule. Let's talk about what we've learned over the past few weeks, and see what we need to adjust in order to still meet our objective."

The outcomes of these kinds of sessions can be three-fold. First, you can conclude on the basis of new knowledge that the original objective was unrealistic, and re-specify it. Second, you can conclude that, though still a stretch and maybe even more of one than you thought previously, there are some adjustments that you can make to keep the original commitment in sight. Third, you can conclude that the commitment is realistic, but not for the team that had been assembled. The answer in that instance is to adjust the team, which may involve reassignments or replacements, and go on.

Regardless of the outcome, if you handle it this way you will have given people time to learn and adjust. You will have been open to new thinking. You will have been a valid contributor to the solution. And you will have maintained your responsibility for the result. People will respect you for that. You will have a far greater prospect of achieving extraordinary results. And, finally, you will sleep well.

Kindness

What's the highest return investment you can make in your business? I believe that it's your own kindness. Kindness takes no more time than unkindness. Generally, it requires no outlay of funds. The impact of your kindness on other peoples' confidence, on their willingness to "go the extra mile" for you, and on the resulting responsibility they feel to you and to the business are huge.

Why is it, then, that so many people running businesses don't build kindness into their ways of being while at work? Why is it that our mental picture of the person in charge so often includes a furrowed brow, piercing eyes, tight lips, and a generally unpleasant expression? How many people really look forward to spending an hour with the president? In how many businesses would most employees find that hour to be an entirely enjoyable event? Very few, in my experience. But those few have something special in common, which usually has a lot to do with the individual in charge being seen as a generally kind person.

Being kind doesn't mean that you avoid the hard issues. It doesn't mean that you are less than demanding, or that you behave like a wimp. It doesn't mean that you don't say what needs to be said, when it needs to be said. Nor does it mean that you would put anything ahead of your interest in, or your responsibility for, the well-being of your business. I've fired people, even for cause, but have done it in as kind a way as I thought possible, and have felt great about it. They felt better than if it had been done otherwise. Everyone who heard about it was favorably disposed. And we avoided further entanglements.

The key to handling yourself this way is to bring to all of your responsibilities the conscious intention to do what needs to be done in a way that is respectful of other peoples' rights to work out their own good lives as well as they can, and in a way that is respectful of their needs to feel as good about themselves as they can under the circumstances. Do this even for your enemies.

In kindness, there's no room for ego, for revenge, for plotting downfalls, for talking behind the back, or for gloating over the misfortune of another. As much as we, as a group, might relish the thought of destroying our competition, I'd rather have my company thinking about maximizing the quality of life for ourselves, and letting the other chips fall where they may.

Most of kindness is so easy that it feels a little foolish even writing about it. It should be indelible in our subconscious. It's the friendly hello in the morning. It's asking if you can bring anything back for someone while you're out. It's listening intently to what someone else has to say. It's signing birthday cards. It's acknowledging when someone's family member is having a rough time. It's attending funerals. It's knowing people's names and what their kids are doing. It's taking the time to write thank-you notes. It's just being seen as a nice but firm and thoughtful person. And it's incredible how quickly these tiny gestures spread through a company and how quickly they add up.

Every now and then, however, there comes along an opportunity to do something extraordinary in the name of kindness. I always look hard for these opportunities because they set such a powerful example for others and they convey the idea of kindness with resounding volume.

One of the better stories I've experienced involved the CEO of a construction firm in the Southeast nearly thirty years ago. He was notoriously no-nonsense and tough, but was also a revered and a fair man. I was with him in a board meeting when he was interrupted to take a telephone call. Without a word of explanation, he hung up the receiver and left the room. Later that day, we all learned that there had been an accident on a power plant job. An hourly laborer was trapped beneath a collapsed section of foundation wall thirty feet below grade. We got no further reports that day.

By the next afternoon, the story was coursing the halls about the CEO arriving on the job site in exactly what he was wearing when he left the boardroom, an elegant gray nail-head suit with black cap-toe shoes. We discovered that after he left the meeting, he had headed for the airport and taken his seat at the controls of the company helicopter. Once at the site, he donned a hard hat, descended into the muddy pit, cap-toed English shoes and all, and cradled the laborer's head until he was extracted seven hours later, around 11:00 pm.

A year later, the story was that the CEO had held the laborer's head for twelve straight hours. Two years later, it was two days. Such is the power of the lore of extraordinary kindness.

Generosity

We usually think about generosity as the act of giving away things. Material things. That's not the thrust of what we're talking about here. I'm talking more along the lines of generosity of spirit. Generosity of spirit is about the way we think about other people.

Sadly, today it's easy to find people we wouldn't characterize as overly generous. Others have already written and talked about why this is the case. All you have to do is watch the local evening news. We see too many television news stories and read too many headlines about people doing terrible things to others. While I continue to hold a strong belief that human beings are innately generous, there's much evidence to the contrary. I believe that, as a result of the barrage of negative stories, many of us have been conditioned out of generosity as a wonderful way of approaching the world, and we use cautiousness and suspicion as a tactic for survival.

Call me corny, but I believe that generosity is a value worth preserving, and there are only a few positions left in our society from which it can be practiced, in an appropriate degree of moderation, with high visibility for others and with relatively little risk. One of these positions is head of a business.

Over the past few years I've consciously tried to build generosity into the way I think about other people. When people tell me something, my first response is to do my best to believe them. Then I try to work from the expectation that what they have told me is truthful and that they are reliable.

I don't get disappointed very often. Most of the time, people tell me their best version of the truth. I think the fact that they know I am giving them the benefit of the doubt makes them less inclined to take me on snipe hunts. But on occasion, some do. In those rare instances, the effects usually aren't too bad, and I don't hesitate to deliver an immediate, fair reprimand in such a way that others see and appreciate the consequences of deceit.

On the whole, I get a lot more pleasure out of looking at others through a generous and positive set of lenses. I find that once others catch on, and after a few exposures, they begin to do the same. Before too long, your conscious commitment to generosity can change a culture of suspicion and game-playing into a culture of trust, openness, and confidence—and the risks are not very high.

Humility

There's not much that commends people in seats of power to others more effectively than their own humility. If you are running the business, you don't need to put on any airs to be noted as someone special. It's already clear to everyone that you are. Emphasizing the point serves no one's interest but your own, and then for only a short while. The fruit of hubris is nearly always disdain.

So why do so many people in positions of power act the way they do? I have two thoughts. My first thought is that they don't know any better. The other leads me to assign responsibility to a manager they've watched run a business without humility in the past, upon whom they've imprinted.

One of my most loved and now-deceased colleagues once told me that the most significant factor in shaping a businessperson's demeanor for the entirety of his career is the demeanor of his first boss. If yours was a jerk, you're likely to be one too! As much as I loved my old friend and mentor, I never was entirely satisfied with his explanation on this particular point. It's not that I dispute his logic—I think it's probably true in many instances. But I was looking for something more. Something more fundamental. Why, for example, was the first boss a jerk?

The answer lies unswervingly with a shortfall of self-confidence. People who lack self-confidence have a hard time being humble, particularly when they find themselves in highly visible positions where they are afraid that someone might find out that they're just not carrying all the goods. Brusqueness and arrogance are convenient ways of keeping people at a distance. And if you are the one in charge, you might be able get away with it, largely because people will be afraid of you. But they will never respect you. They will never give you their consummate all. And you will be setting a bad example for everyone in your wake.

Think about it this way. What if you are in charge? Does that make you any better than anyone else? There's a high likelihood that, because of the complexity of your responsibilities, you are, in fact, actually worse at your job than most other employees are at theirs, no matter how good you are. And, believe me, people see through pretenders.

So, the chances are high that you aren't as good at your job as you ought to be, and the odds are similarly high that everyone else knows it. The worst thing that you can do in this situation is to attempt a charade. You'll look like a fool. But the worst part is that no one will let you know it. They'll talk behind your back, but never to your face. You'll become one of those unfortunate "downers" that most employees just have to put up with during the course of their average, uninspiring day at work. And again, worst of all, they'll never let you know. Can you see yourself against the standard of humility as a "downer"? Don't feel bad. From time to time we all are. Just don't get too accustomed to being that way or you will lose your followers for good.

It's far better to be open, honest, and approachable. Be first to take the blame and last to take the credit. While people feign reverence in the presence of an arrogant president, they love a humble one. While they might follow a self-serving one lifelessly and grudgingly, they'll dance their hearts out in the path of the one with whom they can relate. Humility is simply seeing yourself as no better than others, and acting accordingly. You get no special parking places, no right to cut in line, no preference for the company football tickets. You serve hot dogs at the company picnic, eat in the company lunchroom, and use the plant restroom. And you are openly willing to take all of the responsibility for things that go wrong and to give all of the credit to others when they go right.

Remember, your hopes for health, your dreams for your kids, your aspirations to spend your later years comfortably with your life partner, and your desire to make a difference for others are no different from those of your most recently hired and lowest-paid employee. Why, then, should you act any different?

Courtesy

What happened to manners? A good friend who is an attorney moved recently from his native Boston, a city he'd seldom left even for vacations, to Atlanta. After a couple of weeks I rang him up to see how he was settling in.

I asked what most surprised him about the South. Before I could finish the last two words of my question, he blurted out, "Manners!" I guess there's a natural gap between taking note of something new and attractive, and being able to practice it.

Courtesy is a way of approaching life that is grounded in a desire to make every personal encounter a pleasant one, whether you know the person or not and whether you expect to ever see the person again or not. While kindness is one-on-one, courtesy is social, and it is as much about upholding the tenets of an ennobling code as it is about the instant effect on the recipient. Through our courteous behaviors we inspire others to do the same. Courtesy, therefore, demonstrates a loving way of being for others, which at the same time contributes to the preservation of an overall pleasantness in society.

However, for all its wonderful qualities, courtesy is also a delicate thing, because we find it so easy to overlook its abrogation. We all are witnesses every day to countless acts that are not courteous. They're things that don't necessarily cross the line into discourteousness, but they are acts that could have been done with a much higher regard for pleasantness and weren't. Somehow, for most of us, it's just not worth the extra effort it takes to behave more courteously. The decline of courtesy also finds root in the general twenty-first-century societal desire for personal independence and freedom from discipline. But society without discipline is anarchy. And society without pleasantness is lifeless.

Regardless of cultural trends, however, you can do something about courtesy through your own behavior within the confines of your own world—your business. You can act with courtesy and, importantly, you can let people know that it's important to you. No, you can't fire an employee for minor courtesy violations, but you can let people know when they violate a principle of courtesy and that you expect more of them.

You may be met on your first few tries, as I often have been, with looks of disbelief: "Is he really saying this to me?" After this happened to me a few times, I was shocked to learn that I was the first person who had ever taken the time to point out courtesy to the other person as a desirable attribute, including the teachers they could remember, their parents, and their spouses.

So I go forth undaunted. Even inspired. With a personal sense of mission for courtesy in life at work. I'm not criticizing people, I'm helping them. And you know what? Most people come around quite nicely. They may not respond the first time, but once they figure out that you are serious they will adapt their own behavior. And they respond particularly well to comments like, "Do you know how what you said made me feel?" and "You know, you could have made my whole morning if you had just _____," rather than a general admonition or a sermon on courteous behavior.

Your courtesy campaign will be particularly noted if you're already making progress on most of the other issues we've talked about. Let people see and understand who you are and how you're wired on a few of the other points before you take this one on with a high level of verve. In the meanwhile, just consistently demonstrate courtesy yourself, and you'll be laying important groundwork.

The message here is that you can make a tremendous difference in the culture of your business through conscious attention to courtesy, if you want to. And you already know it. Just think about the times you've entered the reception room of a supplier's or a customer's business and have been met by a well-groomed person with a smile on his face who stands up to greet you, welcomes you warmly, and offers to hang your coat and get you a cup of coffee. Contrast that with a disheveled receptionist, hunched over a coffee-stained spiral notebook behind a piece of glass with a hole in it, who looks up, still chewing on a pencil, and with a vacuous gaze and mutters, "Yeah, whaddaya want?"

One costs no more than the other. Each, however, speaks volumes about the relative degrees of pleasantness that one is likely to experience as an employee, as a customer, or as a supplier in either instance. And the difference starts with rigorous attention to courtesy at the top.

Unselfishness

Most of us think about selfishness, and the lack of it, first in material terms. The whole concept of personal property—its seemingly limited supply, the rights associated with its ownership, and what it takes to get it in our society—conditions people toward selfishness. Complete material unselfishness, therefore, is a very, very tall order, unless you happen to be a member of a monastic order or of a very wealthy commune. In which case the likelihood of you reading this page is very low. But there is quite a valuable distance that the rest of us can span between obsessive self-centeredness and the materially unselfish ideal. I have found that the farther you can get toward the unselfish end of the materialism range, the better you will be at running your business.

Apart from material unselfishness, there is another, and I believe easier, way to think about unselfishness. Making progress along this other route also usually results in progress along the material path. This is mental unselfishness—unselfishness of thought, in contrast to unselfishness of property. While it may be difficult to contemplate not protecting your home, your car, or your bank account, it may be easier to think about giving up your need to think continuously about protecting the overall well-being of yourself before others. This interpretation of unselfishness is a lot closer to intellectual selflessness than material denial, and I've found that it's an easier place to start.

The anchor point for intellectual unselfishness comes back again to one's own sense of security. Where confidence is strong, unselfishness is easy. Where it's weak, it's hard. The people who find it easiest are either older folks who have gotten themselves over the need to "have things," or they are younger people whose parents have given them incredible senses of confidence, security, and self worth. To these kinds of people, the fear associated with losing things or failing in other peoples' eyes is not very great. They've gotten themselves on another plane of self-evaluation that releases them to be more concerned for others than for themselves. It's a wonderful place to be.

The best news is that you don't have to be old or the recipient of extraordinary parenting to get to a place of intellectual unselfishness. In fact, the position of running a business is one of the easiest places to develop this quality, and it's about the most important place for it to exist.

Easiest? Of course it is! As the head of your business, you've already reached a position of prominence. You have courage and intellect that others admire. You have the highest prospects of creating wealth among your colleagues. And you have the potential to make enormous positive differences in other peoples' lives. There is a lot not to be worried about when you are running your business. And with the mind-space that you don't need to focus on yourself, you can focus on others.

Most important? Absolutely. Just like pretensions and airs, self-centeredness and selfishness are very easy for others to read. If you are selfish, you cannot hide it. It's in everything you do. And it's obvious to everyone else. Your clearest signal, however, is from within. Because self-centered and selfish people are never happy. They never have enough. There's always someone with more, and that makes them feel unworthy. It's a terrible burden for the bearer and, much more importantly, for everyone around him.

So, if you are selfish and self-centered, and you likely are to some degree, how do you change? There's no prescription you can take, nor is there a twelve-step program you can follow. It's simply a matter of consciousness and a matter of will. It's about having enough interest in the idea of becoming less selfish and less self-centered, and about a commitment to begin examining your own thinking. It's about aspiring to become continually conscious of not thinking selfishly.

I remember writing "Think of others first" on every page of a new pocket calendar several years ago. It helped. After looking at the message several times a day for a few weeks, I found a new dimension sneaking into my decision making and a new consideration finding its way into my behavior, both of which were very well received by others. With positive reinforcement, it became a source of satisfaction. And it got a lot easier. I found myself gratified not to be thinking about myself all the time. I began to feel less burdened and I built up a new confidence that if I simply stuck to thinking about taking care of others, I would be cared for in return. And from that point forward, the practice of unselfishness has never let me down.

Try it. It's easier that you might think. And you'll like it. Others will too, including your spouse, your kids, your friends, your mother, and the dog. They'll like it a lot.

Good Humor

Professor Drummond wrote beautifully crafted illustrations in support of good humor. He called the reverse, bad humor, "often the singular blot on an otherwise noble character." At another point he described bad humor as "a bubble escaping occasionally to the surface revealing the existence of something rotten below."

Like bad manners, bad humor is one of those unfortunate things that we tend to tolerate. Worse than our acceptance of bad manners, however, our tolerance levels for bad humor seem to correlate with a person's position on the organizational chart, to the point that bad humor seems to have become an unquestioned privilege and even a badge and a symbol of rank. What's most unfortunate about this situation is that most people imprint unconsciously upon whomever they sense is in charge. If the senior managers are ill humored, everybody tends to be. And a place of work where ill humor reigns isn't much fun, or fulfilling. It usually isn't very productive either. In well-led and well-managed businesses, the situation is just the reverse.

I believe that zero tolerance for bad humor is a responsibility of credible leadership. Part of your job is to make more good decisions than bad ones. But another part is to set an example for others to follow that inspires them and makes the time they spend in your business a positive part of their lives. Putting up with your bad humor isn't something that helps others in any way. It reduces their effectiveness and deprives them of the fulfillment that they have a right to expect in return for their efforts to help you.

In an attempt to elevate and to discipline my own good humor, several years ago I began to think about employees, all the people at work, as volunteers. Most of your employees do, in fact, have options. But they have chosen to spend their time at work with your business. So, treat them like you would a volunteer. Your personal demeanor should reflect your gratitude for their choice. All the time. No matter what other weighty matters or disappointments might be on your mind. Maintain your good humor as a reflection of all of your other noble attributes, and show your employees the character and resilience of the person with whom they have chosen to cast their lot.

I find two kinds of bad humor in the highest ranks of business. One is a general sourness that, surprisingly, most people find easier to deal with than the second. The second is volatility—even-temperedness spiked with brief but high-amplitude swings of emotion, which are highly visible to others, some of whom might find themselves unfortunate victims of these outbursts.

Both are bad, but the first, though clearly a spirit dampener, at least is predictable. The second is always more disconcerting. When an employee cannot count on consistency from the leader, he never feels secure and, therefore, is never intellectually and emotionally prepared to give his best. The lack of good humor at the top of businesses promotes timidity in the ranks, and timidity is a cancer to greatness.

Good humor is the salve of success. It puts people at ease. It releases them to do their best. And it makes them want to do it, for you. So, what do you do if you blow it? Lose your cool and yell a while? Moving ahead as if it never happened or as if you don't care that it did are the worst alternatives. Though it may be hard for you, a public apology works best. The public apology does two things. First, because it is embarrassing, it's good self-discipline for you. Second, people will respect you for it.

But what if you have been living a life pattern at work for a long time that is continually sour or volatile? Wouldn't an apology be so out of character that it might have an even worse effect? Probably so, unless you do one additional thing. That is to let people know that you've been reading and thinking about how you could do your job better, because they deserve it, and that you've decided to focus on good humor. This apology is your first step, and you hope that everyone will support you in your effort. If you can muster up the courage to do this and if you mean it, they won't just respect you, eventually they'll clap, they'll cheer, and they will love you for making the change. People have an amazing way of encouraging what they want, and of forgetting about what they don't want.

Guilelessness

Guile, as Drummond described it, is suspicion for suspicious people. Guilelessness is not having this trait. This is one of the more complicated of the nine attributes of love for many people. In one regard, it's similar to generosity of spirit—in its orientation toward giving others the benefit of the doubt—but it's much more deliberate and more rigorous in the way it actually plays out.

We've all been conditioned since childhood to be on constant alert in our dangerous world for those who would harm us. Our training starts early, with warnings as universal and as innocuous as, "Don't talk to strangers." By adulthood, this kind of conditioning has built into most of us a "healthy" wariness of others that serves as an instinct for personal survival.

The difficulty with maintaining a "healthy" suspicion of others as part of our approach to life, however, is that, when dealing with others, we usually get what we expect. Involuntarily, we signal our distrust to others in ways that trigger them to behave in like fashion toward us. It fosters a sort of dance of suspicion that keeps us from giving one another as much of ourselves as we might, if we were not so suspicious and defensive. But, still, no one wants to be a patsy. So most of us conclude that it's simply better to live out our relationships with other people according to the "safe, not sorry" axiom. This minimizes our risk, but also minimizes our return from our interactions with others. Quite a dilemma.

Guilelessness, practiced well, lets us have it both ways. It's a way of committing fully to people and not getting burned in the process. In contrast to generosity, which becomes an unconscious way of going about life, guilelessness is much more intentional. It's a controlled pattern of behavior that maximizes the prospects that you'll get the most out of your association with people you don't know very well, while consciously protecting yourself from the occasional outlier.

How does it work? It starts with a general attitude of optimism regarding other people. It's a belief that people are fundamentally good. It's also the belief that badness is temporary and that, given enough time—again, for some it may be up until their last breath—people eventually reform. Even when the first signals aren't good, effective guilelessness starts with a willingness to give other parties the benefit of the doubt and to look for signals of their goodness rather than for confirmation that they're bad.

The next step comes if you are disappointed. The key here is to deal with transgressions unemotionally (no "How could you let me down?" speeches), immediately, and constructively. I find that something along these lines usually works: "Because I care about you and want things to work out well between us, I have to let you know that what you just did is not acceptable and cannot be tolerated around here." If that speech provokes an excuse, I usually just listen. Don't allow yourself to get drawn into argument. When the employee is finished, I usually respond, again unemotionally, with something like, "Regardless of the circumstances, what you did was hurtful to the business and to others. Again, I want things to work out well for you, and I will help you, but if another infraction occurs, we'll be parting ways." Justice is a part of love, and delivering justice is a much more considerate act, though a much more difficult one, than ignoring something when you know it's wrong.

And finally, because situations vary in terms of acceptable timeframes for the conversion to goodness—sometimes you can wait, and other times you can't—set a milestone for everyone who needs one, and let the employee know about it. Without being judgmental, you can tell someone who isn't toeing your line that she has until a specific date to turn things around, and that you will give her all the help and encouragement she might need. But you also must let her know that if things don't improve by the date specified, or if another infraction occurs in the meanwhile, that you wish her all the best, however she will be leaving. There should be no emotion, no grudge, no power trip on your part. You are just doing what you need to do, both for your business and for the other person, because you believe in the principle of fairness and because you care about all of your employees.

Personally, I've had things like this work out a hundred different ways, but when I've followed the general principles and outline for guilelessness, they've all been okay. The best, of course, are the turnaround cases. The people whom nobody thinks will make it, but who, due to your guilelessness, turn out to be the model colleagues. These people make you feel great. You'll remember their faces as the best parts of your career. And they will love you for it forever.

Sincerity

The people who are best at running businesses are also open, approachable, thoughtful, genuinely interested in you, and authentic—they are sincere. You know when you are in the presence of someone who is sincere. Sincere people are incredibly good at listening, they look you in the eye, and when the discussion is over, you feel like you got through to them. You feel like you really talked to a person, not to a suit wrapping a caricature of a CEO.

Sincerity is a powerful show of respect for other people. It makes a person feel important and like he is special to you. By dealing with people sincerely, you also make them feel special about themselves. And why wouldn't you want them to feel that way?

Looking back over Drummond's nine principles for the summum bonum, I am reminded of what another one of my most loved mentors was fond of telling me: "Gaining the love of one's people is always an inside job." Live your own life with patience, kindness, generosity, courtesy, humility, unselfishness, good humor, guilelessness, and sincerity, and followership will come to you. Without worrying about it at all.

But there are some tips that help in making sure that your messages are taken for what they are intended to be, and not misunderstood when you deliver them. And all of these tips all have to do with your having a better understanding about how other people think, receive, and processs your messages.

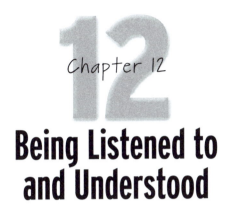

Chapter 12

Being Listened to and Understood

Earlier I noted that people in your organization are watching you, more carefully than you'd ever imagine, for signals about how they can please you. It is imperative, therefore, that you communicate your expectations clearly, consistently, and accurately to them. This communication occurs in two ways. The one we think about most often is verbal communication. The other, which receives much less attention but which is, in fact, much more powerful, is nonverbal communication.

Some of the greatest leaders and managers I've met really haven't been all that smooth as verbal communicators. Some of us are gifted in that regard and others aren't. And the good news is that it doesn't make that much of a difference which part of the gene pool we crawled out of, as long as what comes from us is seen as being in alignment with the principles outlined throughout this book. In fact, facility with words can be a trap. If the speech comes too easily, it's often not thought out as well as it should be. And the essence of what you say is infinitely more important than what you sound like.

Working with the Channels of Communication

From nearly forty years of trial and error in communicating what I need from others and why I need it, in all kinds of business situations, I've learned some things. I also know that the things I've learned, mostly the hard way, are tips that can help all of us to become more effective communicators in our roles running businesses.

A good place to start is to recognize that not everyone is wired the same way when it comes to our preferences for communication and learning. While there are many theories and a whole body of knowledge that has been popularized since World War II, particularly focused on learning patterns of children, the one I like best is not among the best known. It comes from a woman named Dawna Markova, who wrote a book called *How Your Child Is Smart* around 1990. While her focus was on children, she presented a terrifically insightful model for better understanding the differences in our preferences for, and in our facilities with, receiving and processing information.

Markova's theory begins with a hypothesis that feels right. Backed up by some science from neurological experiments, she theorizes that we all use different parts of our brains, which she calls channels, for different kinds of thinking. Our front channel is where we receive, process, and return information in real time, such as when we're talking to someone. Our middle channel is where we solve problems. We use it when we are trying to decide between several alternative courses of action. Our back channel is where we find our creativity. It's also where our deepest and our most personal emotions reside. So, three zones of our brain equal three styles of using it.

Markova notes then that there are also three modes for receiving and sending information—auditory, visual, and kinesthetic. These correspond to hearing, seeing, and doing. Next, and again with scientific backing, she explains that different people seem to have clear preferences for one mode versus the other two in each of the three channels, and that the preferences tend to be mutually exclusive. There's a different, preferred mode per channel.

For example, a person might have an auditory orientation in her front channel, where real-time communication occurs. She receives, processes, and returns verbal information easily in real time. In her middle channel, she might be visually oriented. While problem solving, she sees pictures of the alternatives in her mind. Then, by default, in her back channel, where creative work takes place, she is kinesthetically oriented. To become optimally creative, she might need to take a walk, doodle with a pen, or fidget in her chair. The main point here is that there are a total of thirty-six different patterns that seem to be distributed roughly evenly across the population, and none indicates any higher level of intelligence or potential than another. They're just different wiring patterns. And they affect how each of us best receives and deals with information.

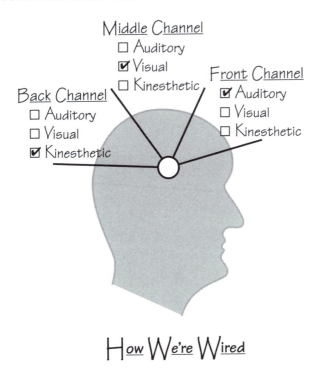

How We're Wired

This is a big idea, and it's one that should be important to you if you want to communicate effectively with everyone in your business. It means, for example, that if you gave everyone in your business a speech you made on a CD, about one third of your audience would be processing what you had recorded. The other two thirds would be getting parts of it, with difficulty, or zoning out. It also means that, because words don't come easily to everyone, those who don't stand out in group discussions aren't necessarily uninterested, uninformed, or unintelligent. And because someone looks out the window or fidgets when you talk to him, he's not necessarily inattentive or disrespectful. In most instances, he's just doing his best to handle his half of what's going on between the two of you. And you should respect it.

I take two key lessons from this. One is that, when you are talking to a group, you should try to cover all three channels. Be clear with your words. Give your audience something to look at. Be animated: Move your hands, walk around a little, change your facial expression, use a prop or two. And finally, let people know that if they need to move around, fidget, doodle, repeat your words silently or look out the window while you are talking, that it's okay. You know that it helps them listen and you won't be offended.

The other lesson has to do with one-on-one interactions. I try to be very conscious about how the people with whom I spend most of my time are wired. I know, for example, that there are some with whom I simply need to talk in order to get my message across. A message left on a smartphone does its job. Even passing messages along through, if the words are right, will work. In yet other cases, I know that I need to give them a fat marker and take one myself, and we need to sit together in front of a whiteboard and draw together while we talk in order for them to get it. And with still others, if I want to get a point across, we need to take a walk.

So, how do you know how others are wired? Simply keeping the explanation and the diagram above in mind usually works. In addition, you can be pretty sure of your diagnosis by attending to the following signals:

- Auditory in the front channel: Interacts in conversations freely, with words that come easily. Enjoys speaking in front of others. Has a great vocabulary and remembers what's been said, and seems riveted to the flow of conversation.
- Visual in the front channel: Seems focused on the things in your office, like a picture on your wall or a trophy on your shelf, or doodles when you speak. Takes copious notes that are well organized and neat, and remembers the details of where she's been.
- Kinesthetic in the front channel: Drums her fingers on your desk. Walks around or rolls her head, stretches her arms and locks her fingers occasionally, and is quick to describe how she feels.

You get to the patterns in the middle channel, the problem-solving zone, by asking simple questions, like, "When we go to Chicago next week, do you have a preference for where we stay?" Then follow up by asking your employee how he came to his decision. Did he imagine the looks or the logos of alternative places? Did he repeat the question to himself? Or did he imagine how he might feel in the room before bed or upon waking?

The back channel preference will be the one left over. A good check on the whole of your diagnosis is to pay close attention to the times when someone loses her train of thought and just spaces out. We all do it. Was it something she saw that distracted her? Or a touch on the shoulder? Or a particular word or phrase? In addition to giving you some confidence in the other parts of your characterization, knowing what triggers this back channel is powerful insight for knowing how to plant an emotional seed— for instance, core values or purpose—deep in another's consciousness where it will reside safely, and for knowing what stimulus to touch to bring it back into play consistently.

With just a little practice this patterning becomes fun, and eventually something you don't even have to think about consciously. After just a minute or two with a new acquaintance, you will pick up the signals and involuntarily adapt your own behaviors in order to be best understood.

Some Other Verbal Communication Tips

In addition to the general advice about paying attention to how people are wired and adapting your own methods to match how they prefer to receive and deal with information, I have listed below specific habits that I've developed over the years. These are reliable tips for maximizing your effectiveness as the head verbal communicator in your business organization:

> Make time to talk to people. Walk around the office and the plant every day for small talk. Invite people into your office. Hold a monthly "lunch with the president" for anyone who is interested.

> Learn everyone's names and comment favorably to others about your employees in their presence.

> Tell the truth. Don't dodge tough questions. When you can't answer a question you're asked, say so. If you think that you can answer it later, tell the person that you'll get back to him, then do it in a timely fashion. Never make up something just to get through an awkward moment. People know it.

Be optimistic, even when things are grim. State the current circumstance as accurately and as honestly as you can, even if it's dire, then tell people what you are going to do about it, and why you think you'll all get through.

Don't hide. When things are darkest, the worst thing you can do is retreat to your office and abandon your team. It is during the times of gravest crisis that you need to be most visible, most inspiring, and most accessible. Position yourself staunchly on the front lines, like General Jackson did, earning for himself the nickname Stonewall.

Be brief. When you've finished saying what you need to say, stop. In most conversations, you are simply conveying information, not selling. People don't like being sold, don't trust the seller, and know when it's happening.

Do your best to look people in the eye when you talk to them. Be aware, however, of cultural differences, particularly if you are heading a company outside your own country or if your workforce is diverse. In many Asian cultures, for example, looking someone in the eye is a sign of disrespect.

Apologize when it's appropriate and do it immediately, either publicly or privately, depending on what's occurred. The inevitable breeches of intention or judgment that you make are best resolved in the instant when you recognize them. Sometimes, by the time you realize your mistake, a lot of other people know of it too. And if they don't already know, they'll respect and trust you for telling them first.

Be consistent. When you know what you're saying is different from what you've said in the past, let people know that you are aware of it, and explain what's changed and why.

Talk over and over again about your vision and strategy. Weave them into every speech and every discussion in which you lead a group to a decision. Justify your decisions in terms of your vision—particularly your core values, purpose, and mission—every time you get the chance. Refer to them in all your writings to your organization, your trade press, and your suppliers.

Practice before you make a speech. Test it out on someone in advance. Record it and listen to it on your phone.

Become the best listener in your company. Avoid the temptation to think about anything but what the speaker is saying to you in the moment. Repeat her main points. Take notes. Summarize the conversation when it's done. And thank her for the time together.

Nonverbal Communication Tips

Because only one third of the people who work for you are likely to be wired for optimal real-time communication through what you say, it stands to reason that nonverbal methods of communication are also worth thinking about and using consciously. Here are some proven tips for using what you don't say to get your messages across to the rest of your universe:

Smile. All the time. You'd be amazed at the harmful impact of a single furtive glance or grimace and how quickly your negative reaction travels through your company. And you'd be amazed how much easier it is for nonverbal people to process your spoken messages if they are put at ease by the image you portray when you are speaking.

Maintain an open stance. Crossing your arms is a signal that you are closed-minded. Having your palms out is a sign of openness and trustworthiness.

Shake hands firmly. People read confidence into handshakes. There are few things less inspiring than a weak handshake from one's leader.

Your eyes are a traitor to your thoughts. Maintain eye contact. Don't try to mask what you are feeling by looking away. It won't work. It's far better to maintain solid eye contact and tell someone what you are feeling.

Put your discussion partner at ease. Mirroring always works. This means that when she leans forward, you do too. When she crosses her legs, so do you. When she looks away, you do too. You might think this is hokey and too obvious. But it's not. Particularly from your position of perceived power, your matching yourself to your employee's presentation unconsciously gives her great comfort and a willingness to be open with you.

Be well groomed, with tidy hair and clean clothes. Pick a style of dress that's appropriate for you and your business, and stick to it. To add a little interest, you can vary your wardrobe within the overall boundaries of the style you've chosen. But pay attention to whether what you wear and how you are groomed lines up with what you've conditioned people to expect from you. People want you to be consistent but interesting within appropriate limits.

Laugh with people. Don't be afraid to kid around with them. You are much more human with a sense of humor, particularly about yourself.

Touching someone in an appropriate way—shaking hands or touching a shoulder—adds depth to relationships.

Do the small things. Pick up after yourself. Wash your own coffee cup. Make your own copies.

Do the unexpected good thing. Surprise people, for no particular reason, every now and then, with something nice for everyone.

Demand a clean workplace. Focus on the lunchroom and on the bathrooms, particularly in the plant. Then work outward.

Show interest in others' work. Have lunch in the plant once a week. Learn to work the machinery. Go on sales and service calls occasionally. Go to department or group meetings every now and then, just to listen and show interest. If your business involves consumer contact, work the counter for a day a few times a year, or accompany a driver on deliveries.

Keep your office tidy. Avoid opulence. Don't have much space, furniture, or amenities that are beyond what other people have. Watch out for too many "golf with the guys" photos. Your space should be all about your work, if you want others' to be about theirs.

Don't drive your extravagant car to work.

Don't have a reserved parking space. If you're late, take what's available and walk. Even if you are first to arrive, don't take the closest spot. Early arrivals will notice if your car is in the middle of the lot away from the door, leaving closer spots for others. And they'll tell others about it, in an exceedingly positive way.

Be the first to celebrate. Rejoice in even the small wins.

Be there in times of need and celebration for your people. Handwrite, don't type, sympathy and congratulation cards. Go to funerals and weddings.

Be one of them—just with a different set of responsibilities at which you are extraordinarily good.

Be fun.

Chapter 13

Special Considerations for New Appointees

There are two kinds of new appointees to the highest posts in organizations: real first timers—people who've never had a chance to run a business before—and situational first timers—people who've been in charge of businesses before but are walking into a new assignment. The advice here for both are surprisingly similar.

The two most important things to keep in mind apply equally in both cases. The first is that everyone who matters expects, and desperately wants, you to be a success. You wouldn't have gotten the job in the first place if this were not the case, and you can be assured that whoever made the hiring decision has already preached your virtues to everyone else. The second thing to keep in mind is that you have a grace period, a honeymoon of sorts, and everyone expects you to take it in order to get yourself oriented.

Remembering these two truths gives you a reliable measure of confidence when you need it at the outset of a new assignment, and you will. They also go a long way toward taking the edge off the feelings of anxiety that everyone walking in as the new person in charge experiences. As the new president or CEO, you have plenty of time to prove yourself. People respect newcomers who take the appropriate time to understand their world. And they are universally offended by an instant know-it-all.

Use your first few weeks to get to know people informally. Decline any suggestions that you give a presentation about who you are, how you run a business, and how glad you are to be there. Let the system carry your messages for now.

Arrange hour- to hour-and-a-half introductory discussions with your key reports in their offices, not in yours or the conference room. Avoid "stacking" these discussions too close together. Don't do more than one a day. And find a way to follow each one with another time together, ideally out of the office, where you demonstrate that you have really thought about what you heard in the first conversation.

Also consider a series of "lunches with the new president" for anyone who wants to attend. Your intention here, and in your initial one-on-one discussions with your key reports, is not to sell yourself or to make proclamations, but rather just to listen to others talk about the business. Don't say anything about your credentials unless you are specifically asked, and then be brief. Be modest and let them know that your real interest lies in learning about them and about the business through their eyes. Use both of these venues to set the expecation that any changes you make will be for the good of the business, and that people whose intentions and capabilities are aligned with that objective have nothing to worry about. Also let them also know that you will not hesitate to make decisions that need to be made on behalf of the business in a timely fashion. Be clear that your decisions will be made in accordance with the principles of fairness, integrity, and respect.

Spend at least a quarter of your days over the first month walking and talking in the hallways and on the plant floor, the warehouse, or your business's equivalent—the important thing is to engage people where they work. Show interest in what they are doing. Ask hundreds of questions. Write down the answers, along with people's names.

Caring enough to record what they say in your first encounters raises their commitment to help you. Study your notes at night so that you can recognize employees by name the next day. Present yourself as an insatiable and enthusiastic learner about all aspects of the business. The only hole you'll fill with a "been there, done that attitude" is the one in which your own insecurity rests. Introducing yourself as a novice about your new business, no matter how much you may already know about it, allows you to begin seeing the important things more quickly. It's particularly helpful in familiarizing yourself with, and in sorting through, current company wisdom for how to make things better. And it gives the people upon whom your success will depend an opportunity to begin to get comfortable with you and to decide that they want to help you.

Avoid disclosing your thoughts about the business at this time, except positive ones. Ask people what they think, and let them know that it will be a while before you form your own opinions. You can assure them, however, that you wouldn't be there if you did not believe that there was a good fit and an attractive outlook, for yourself and for everyone else.

At the same time, you need to be on the lookout for what I call the "Imperial Embrace." Someone will try this maneuver, and you need to be ready for it. In British society the Imperial Embrace has evolved into high art, and I first experienced it when I was a young consultant working directly with the CEO of a UK-based petroleum company. It is the practice of an employee, usually a mid- to upper-tier executive who feels risk in his position, either before or because of your arrival, attempting to develop a special relationship with an influential newcomer like yourself or with an outsider whom he perceives might have special influence at the top. The intention is to establish a personal obligation that gives the embracer special status or access to privileged information that might protect him from consequences others might suffer. It usually takes the form of a special invitation, a gift, or the sharing of a special secret by the embracer.

As opposed to blatant attempts to curry favor, the Imperial Embrace usually takes the form of someone doing something special for you with the hope of establishing some unspecified recognition in return. In the worst cases, your inadvertent complicity can evolve into a form of emotional, rather than transactional, bribery. And some people are very skilled in maneuvering you into these circumstances.

In the United States some of the most obvious clues to look for early in your arrival are:

- Attempts to engage you in discussions that discredit another's skills, traits, or behaviors. In your discussions with your key reports and others, stick to the issues of the business. Deflect these attempts to stray toward evaluations of other employees—and you will get them—with clear signals that your interest is centered for now on the big issues of the business and not on people.

- Advances to share things that the embracer can't share with others. This is a big red flag and one of the classics of the tactic. Here, the embracer usually expresses great relief that you are on board, because there are some things that your predecessor wouldn't deal with and that others won't tell you about that you need to know. To discourage this behavior, let your embracer know that you will be taking notes so that you can share his observations at the next gathering of your team.

- A third tactic is to request that you intervene in an irregularity, which might be as simple as a customer who is upset over a missed order or as complex as evaluating a proposal for a major investment. It is natural for newly appointed CEOs and presidents to seek in their early days an opportunity to make a difference, to demonstrate their value, and to confirm positive expectations about them. Yet, caving into this natural craving can be a grave mistake, particularly when the object of the intervention isn't your own idea but someone else's. Acting immediately on someone else's agenda has the effect of undermining others' confidence in your independence, with the corollary effect of demonstrating that you are vulnerable to court politics. The deflection in this instance, another you surely will face, is simply to ask, "Who is responsible for what you are requesting, and isn't this their job?" Follow up with a question like, "Is there anything else you would like to share that doesn't involve your views on someone else's performance?"

It is the rare new appointee who is steeled to the advances of the skilled Imperial Embracer, but you need to be. And your best defense is to remember that your job is to establish the first drafts of the Back of the Envelope and Vision–Strategy–Execution frameworks for your new business, and that the other things you need to do will become evident through that effort. If you do this initial planning well, eventually you will have your entire organization aligned behind you and committed to what you all need to do.

Once you've made enough headway in your early-stage thinking about your Back of the Envelope and Vision–Strategy–Execution models to feel like you are getting to know your business and your team, and have gotten yourself completely familiar with the arithmetic of your business, it's time to get to know your banker, your accountant, your lawyer, and any other key service providers to your business, including your advertising agency, your consulting engineers, your recruiting agency, and so on. Spend one-on-one time with them and with your board members. Again, listen for their views on the business and for clues that will add to your own emerging ideas. For now, keep your Back of the Envelope and Vision–Strategy–Execution plans for your new business private.

Your next move is to get to know your key customers. Ask your sales manager, if you have one, to give you a rundown on who they are. Study their businesses on the web, learn their organizational structures, and review their past business with you. Then send personal letters, not e-mails but letters—handwritten messages are best—to each of them and ask to schedule a visit. Sign the letters yourself. Then call, yourself, to make the appointments in which you will proceed as you have for your other one-on-one meetings, listening and taking notes without advancing your own views. Present yourself as wanting to develop a complete understanding of your new business, and again incorporate everything you hear into your Back of the Envelope and Vision–Strategy–Execution frameworks.

Attention to this kind of detail when managing your transition into your new assignment serves many purposes. First, it's your opportunity to assure your customers that your showing up doesn't portend any bad effects for them. Second, it's your opportunity to see through their eyes how well your business is doing, particularly in comparison with your rivals. And finally, it's your opportunity to identify something, quickly, with low risk of failure, and with low risk of collateral damage, that you can alert the other members of your team to do to improve your business—and that is to be seen by your own team as the signal of a person of action, but one who is not particularly interested in the center stage, but rather sees her job as helping everyone else be more effective. And finally, it's your opportunity to do something, quickly, with low risk of failure, and with low risk of collateral damage, to improve your business with them—and that is to be seen by them and by your own team as a person of action with something positive to contribute.

All of this might take six to eight weeks, barring any major crises that divert your attention. At the end of this transition period, you should have your own private draft of a Back of the Envelope and Vision–Strategy–Execution framework for your new business. And if you are like me, you will feel a great temptation to begin sharing it with others. Don't! It still needs work. Lots of it. And in order to have the greatest impact when it emerges, it needs to come not from you but from your team.

Your purpose in using the framework in this early going is simply to help you categorize and arrange the entire collection of new things you will be learning into an early draft of the story of your business. This early draft will be a measure against which you can begin testing new things you will be learning and will help you pattern your interactions in such a way that your staff will soon begin to understand how you think. And they will begin imprinting on it.

I usually like to "keep my powder dry"—keep my Back of the Envelope and Vision–Strategy–Execution thinking private—for the first sixty to ninety days. Though the temptation for sharing is a strong one, I continue to be amazed how the story continues to grow in depth, richness, and quality if I simply have the patience to let it unfold for me. And for me alone, for a while.

What happens next? At around the two- to three-month mark, I am ready to begin introducing my team to the Back of the Envelope and Vision–Strategy–Execution frameworks and facilitating their journey through the logic according to the guidelines I described in chapters 2 and 3.

You might be asking, What is the value of secrecy surrounding your thought process, as your plans come into focus? The answer is threefold.

First, you want to be seen as someone who helps everyone else be better than they could be without you. Giving them your answer won't get you there. In fact, the reverse usually happens. Your team will see your story as yours, and will leave you to finish and amend it as your own if you "sell it" to them, rather than let them convolve it for themselves.

Second, no matter how hard you try, you won't get it right by yourself. Your team's honest belief that you are relying on them and upon their wisdom always produces insights that others, including you, will miss, sometimes with grave consequences.

And third, your having your own private draft of a Back of the Envelope and Vision–Strategy–Execution framework for you new business will help you guide your team toward a productive and satisfying use of their time—both the time when you do reveal your frameworks and afterward.

And if you do it well, in the moment when you introduce your frameworks, a great "Aha, that explains a lot" exclamation will rise, and everyone will be anxious to join you for the remainder of the journey.

I truly believe that following this path greatly improves the odds that you will be successful in your endeavor, and that it sets in place a cornerstone for a culture and a following that you cannot achieve in any other way.

Chapter 14

Seeing Your Business in the Context of History

Throughout this book, from the first few pages to the last chapter, I've made the argument that what you need in order to run your business well is a proven framework—a Back of the Envelope plan and a Vision–Strategy–Execution Model—for simplifying the huge body of thinking that already exists about leadership and management in order to apply it to your circumstances.

The final element in that body of knowledge is a general familiarity with the history of businesses like yours. I find a genealogy of sorts helpful for occasional reference and for a background context in thinking about the big picture. Knowing something about history generally makes us stronger in dealing with current circumstances, and following is a very brief overview of business history that you can reference in your job running a mainstream company.

The Era of Business as Craft

Around the time of America's founding, the center of most business was the independent tradesman, an individual who had acquired the skills to make something or perform a service that other people wanted and that they preferred not to do for themselves. The individual tradesman was a complete unit of production, working mostly alone and using hand tools to create a product—glass, a barrel, a gun. The few larger businesses that existed were simply collections of individual tradesmen, each doing mostly the same things to create similar products, backed up by an apprenticeship system that provided support for the more menial tasks and that ensured the proper training of tradesmen for the future.

Many businesses still work this way, and there is nothing wrong with this model. Many of us, in fact, long for the simpler life of the country doctor, the blacksmith, or the turn-of-the-century architect. But for most of us, the complexities of modern life have imposed other dimensions, beyond the plying of one's own trade, which must be taken into account in order to create and sustain a business, even according to the simplest of constructions. Today, for example, the pace of technology requires aggressive, continuous training, research, and development in many businesses. Responsibilities for the environment, health, and safety occupy time and require new processes and technologies in nearly every mainstream business. And the evolution of social networking has introduced another whole set of knowledge and resources, tangential to whatever is produced and sold, that has become the most important differentiator between success and failure in many mainstream businesses.

The Era of Mass Production

When interchangeable parts were perfected and the assembly line was introduced in the early twentieth century, the nature of business changed fundamentally. And while the age of the craftsperson yielded only slowly to the age of factories and machines, especially outside the big cities, the bell of progress had tolled and it would not be unrung.

At the center of the concept of mass production was an uncoupling of the creation of goods from dependence on skilled individuals. The historical unit of production, a person, became an input to production, and one that was more fungible and less significant than the machines and processes he tended.

The production theory fostered an approach to running a business that focused not on celebrating the ingenuity of humans but on protecting the business from it. Frederick Taylor, writing in the early 1900s, pioneered ideas about the standardization of jobs and behavior at work. His theories fit neatly with principles of manufacturing processes, where variance—the kind inherent in human nature—is the greatest enemy of efficiency.

While we've come a long way from Taylor in understanding the potential of people to contribute to business efficiency, many of the fundamental ideas, like the "routinization" of work and minimizing process variance, still play central roles in the operations of even the most progressively managed businesses.

The Era of the Science of Management

Mass production and the application of "routinization" got an enormous boost through the World War I and World War II experiences, particularly through the stateside effort to support victory during the latter conflict. For six years, the best and brightest from both government and industry collaborated to discover ways to exploit mass production, and launched a war-support economy with unprecedented scope, speed, and capacity.

Coming out of those years, business scholars digested the experiences of government and its contractors and enthusiastically retooled their concepts for universal applications across the whole of American commercial enterprise. The result was an entirely new body of thinking, much broader than Taylor's, about how to maximize efficiencies in large-scale production and in all of the other aspects of business organizations and infrastructure that support it—which became known collectively as the science of management.

Heretofore, the "science" of business had been more akin to the softer social sciences than to the hard physical sciences. But the amazing experiences of the war-time economy spawned the idea of applying the rigors of hard science methodology—of hypothesis development, experiment design, measuring and monitoring, statistical analysis of results, and interpretive evaluation—to the realm of business scholarship. By the mid-1960s there was a growing belief that in business, as in nature, there are prevailing rules, and that by applying scientific principles one could discover them and win.

The Era of Financial Engineering

Through the late 1950s and early 1960s, the financial part of this new science of management began to outdistance the other disciplines—manufacturing, human and organizational behavior, business law, and sales and market-ing—in terms of its importance in the eyes of the general management. This happened, I believe, largely because of its importance to capital sources.

The emergence and convergence of math-based decision sciences, econometric modeling methods, inexpensive computational power, and improved communications added fuel to a growing confidence that, "with enough numbers, you can run anything." And for a while, through the 1960s and well into the '70s, this philosophy seemed to work. Multi-business conglomerates sprung rapidly from a maelstrom of merger and acquisition activity. The stock markets bestowed handsome rewards on holding companies that demonstrated the ability to apply the new financial methods and models across ever-expanding portfolios of entirely unrelated enterprises.

The Era of Strategy

Concurrent with the rise of financial engineering as the driving force in businesses logic, another group of leading and widely respected business scholars was rethinking the principles and lessons from their experiences with strategy in support of the war efforts. The premise they raised was that science, no matter how good it may be, proves at times insufficient, on its own, to ensure business success. However, when the best of science is complemented by a better understanding of the terrain and a fuller profile of the enemy, the troops can enter the field with a battle plan that increases the likelihood of victory while embodying the least possible risk.

In the early 1970s, new ideas about the application of military strategy to business combined with ideas from the science of management to yield a fresh, immediately appealing, and logical approach to running businesses, which spawned an explosion of corporate investment in strategic plan-ning departments and expensive consultants. Big businesses pinned their hopes on assembling the best and the brightest to develop strategic plans and operating models that would lead them to success in the increasingly competitive world of business.

The Era of Human Capital

In the 1980s a challenge arose to the pervasive strategic and scientific approach to running companies. I recall a *Business Week* cover from that time that proclaimed in bold red letters, "Strategy Is Dead." The article analyzed the performance of the strategy icons of the Western world and concluded that their spending over the past decade and a half hadn't paid off. Clever and elegant ideas abounded, but few could be tied directly to paybacks. I remember reading the article and thinking it unfair. The idea of strategy was not wrong or irrelevant, but businesses hadn't yet figured out how to use it in meaningful ways.

In the wake of strategy's "death," there surfaced a renewed attention to what had been left behind in the management scientists' zeal for strategy—the organization below the executive suite. The shortcomings of "ivory tower" strategies, coupled with a recognition of the benefits of better workforce education and involvement, were calling into question the very canons for running businesses that had elevated science and strategy to the status of "near natural law" in the minds of many scholars and practitioners over the previous thirty years.

Maybe, instead of running businesses rigidly according to the science of numbers and the logic of detailed strategies, the role of the persons in charge should be to create circumstances and processes that allowed each area of the business to be run from the place it could best be run, usually from the place where the work is performed. In this view, a mixture of insights travelled from the plant floor up, rather than exclusively from the boardroom down, and the business drew on the most appropriate tools from the entire "kit" of business thinking, within an overall system that could capture the best contributions from every individual while avoiding chaos.

The Era of Information Power and Lean

With dramatic reductions in the cost of computational power and with universal, convenient, and entertaining access to knowledge and facts through the Internet came a wave of interest around the power of personalized information. Our current infatuation with personal computers, networked access, smartphones, and the like, is such that the lion's share of many peoples' days at work is spent tending screens, like people used to tend machines five decades ago.

What can be known is now limitless. But what's still missing is our capacity to understand, particularly in mainstream businesses, how much of the limitless resource actually makes a meaningful difference in the performance of our businesses. Until we learn to make swift and unerring judgments about the usefulness of knowledge, we risk losing our focus on the things that really matter and our sense of what ends we are trying to accomplish at work.

On my walks through many mainstream businesses these days, I see too many people mesmerized by their computer screens, neither understanding nor particularly concerned about whether what they are doing is contributing to the well being of the business. A solid and widespread understanding of the Back of the Envelope and Vision–Strategy–Execution frameworks fills this void and adds meaning to employees' work. Keeping these frameworks always in mind greatly reduces the risk that staff will spend valuable time and energy performing tasks that make no difference to the business's goals, even as it increases the likelihood of meaningful ingenuity arising from its most likely sources—where the work is performed.

Although usually ranked behind improving productivity as the objective of lean, I believe that adding meaning to work and anchoring activities in a clear understanding of how they contribute to the health of the business is a crucial outcome. In fact, investing work with meaning is what makes increased productivity possible. Without conscious recognition of this effect, lean risks becoming just another "going through the motions" exercise that people do only because someone higher in the organization wants them to do it.

But arising from, and coupled with, compelling Back of the Envelope thinking and Vision–Strategy–Execution understanding, the lean philosophy helps everyone decide which pieces of information, among the ever-expanding supply, are the most worthwhile. Combined with the kinds of leadership, followership, and management that extend from Back of the Envelope and Vision–Strategy–Execution exercises, lean creates an optimal environment for success.

Postscript

It is exactly at this moment in history that *Just Run It!* and what you now have learned from it fit in. My intention in writing this book has been to give you a framework for using everything at your disposal to run your mainstream business in a way that is profitable and meaningful to everyone it touches, and in a way that is most rewarding to you in all aspects of your life.

Over what takes most people about six hours to read, I have told you about a lot of the most important things I have learned from three decades of running and advising what I call, with deep admiration and affection, our mainstream businesses.

In looking back over what I've written, I see that a lot of it, in fact most of it, looks like common sense. And running a mainstream business does indeed demand common sense and common decency, coupled with uncommon passion and a commitment to do your job well. But the fact remains that most of the things in this book are not in the forefront of our minds as much as they ought to be.

My hope is that, as you carry yourself forward in your position of responsibility through your days at work, this book will serve as a steady reminder and as a reference. I hope that it will be a reminder of the importance of your job. I hope that it will serve as a framework—through the Back of the Envelope and in the Vision–Strategy–Execution models—for thinking about the totality of your responsibility, and for engaging others in your success. I hope that it will serve as a guide to the overarching motivations that lead successful business heads to contribute positively to the lives of everyone they and their businesses touch. And finally, I hope that it will serve you as a portfolio of anecdotes and "war stories," which you are free to use as your own, and which you will recall and pass along to others.

But this book is not over. Because your job of becoming as good as you can be is not over. Whether you are preparing for your first assignment as a president or CEO or are a seasoned veteran, running your business well is a life's work of continuous learning and growth, learning and growth that you need to attend to, consciously, every day.

In this particular regard, I often find myself looking back on things I've done, as recently as a few weeks ago, that I would give almost anything to be able to do again, to do differently, and to do better. Why? Because what we do is important. Because what we do is relentlessly challenging. Because the circumstances, standards, and techniques for what we do are constantly changing. And because what we do deserves to be done better than any of us will ever be able to do it.

So on behalf of all the people who will benefit from you being as good as you can be, thank you for reading this book. I enjoyed writing it for you. And good luck.

Index

What's Next?

If you have enjoyed *Just Run It!* I invite you personally to keep the experience alive. There are a number of ways we can do that. They all start with a visit to DickCross.com.

There you will find:

Free Templates

- Directions for downloading *Free Back of the Envelope and Vision Templates* that you can complete and send back to me. I'll review your submittal and periodically will select one to feature on the website. If yours is chosen, we'll spend an hour on the phone talking about your business.

Summits

- A schedule of upcoming ***Just Run It!* Summits**, where I meet with owners and CEO's to share new war stories and techniques, and to explore other aspects of running an exceptional business.

Training

- Descriptions of structured training in ***Just Run It!*** methods and techniques for yourself, your entire company, or your association group.

Speaking

- Samples of *Presentations* that I can give to your company or your industry group.

Volume Discounts

- Instructions for ordering multiple copies for your employees, family or friends with *Volume Discount Pricing*, coupled with *Free Speaking Engagements and Private Summits* on larger orders.

Consulting

- Personal support from me and my team in transitioning you and your organization into a ***Just Run It!*** success story.

Truly, I hope that the time you have taken to read ***Just Run It!*** is only the beginning of our relationship.